*Economic
Models
and
Methodology*

ECONOMIC MODELS AND METHODOLOGY

Randall G. Holcombe

CONTRIBUTIONS IN ECONOMICS AND ECONOMIC HISTORY,
NUMBER 99

GREENWOOD PRESS
New York • Westport, Connecticut • London

HB135
·H63
1989

Library of Congress Cataloging-in-Publication Data

Holcombe , Randall G.
    Economic models and methodology / Randall G. Holcombe.
        p. cm.—(Contributions in economics and economic history,
  ISSN 0084–9235 ; no. 99)
    Bibliography: p.
    Includes index.
    ISBN 0–313–26679–4 (lib. bdg. : alk. paper)
    1. Economics—Mathematical models. I. Title. II. Series.
  HB135.H63 1989
  330'.01' 5118—dc20   ^ 89–7495

British Library Cataloguing in Publication Data is available.

Library of Congress Catalog Card Number: 89–7495
ISBN: 0–313–26679–4
ISSN: 0084–9235

First published in 1989

Greenwood Press, Inc.
88 Post Road West, Westport, Connecticut   06881

Printed in the United States of America

The paper used in this book complies with the
Permanent Paper Standard issued by the National
Information Standards Organization (Z39.48–1984).

10 9 8 7 6 5 4 3 2 1

To Ross

CONTENTS

PREFACE

Anyone actively engaged in academic research must consider, implicitly if not explicitly, the methodology that provides the foundation for that research. Why does a particular method lead to knowledge and insight, and why is the method chosen by a particular researcher more likely to lead to fruitful results than alternative methods? Answers to these types of questions must guide the researcher in the selection of the methods that will be used in the research project. Methodological questions can be dealt with in a simple and superficial way, to be sure. A researcher might use a particular method because others in the field use it, or perhaps even because it is the only way that the researcher knows how to deal with the problem. And such a cavalier treatment of methodological issues may not be bad. Why should one agonize over how to generate results when there is a tried and true method readily available? However, my informal discussions with colleagues lead me to believe that most of them have given serious consideration to the methods that they use in search of knowledge.

The methodology of economics is not my own primary area of research interest, but like most of my colleagues, I have given more than passing thought to the methodology that I use in my research. Also like most of my colleagues, the methodology I use is pretty much the same as what is generally used in economics, so the thought I have given to my own methodology applies to economic methodology in general. Why do the methods I use lead to knowledge and insight? Why do I choose particular methods over alternatives? This book provides my answers to these questions, organized in what I hope is a logical and persuasive manner. As such, this is not an encyclopedia of economic methodology, but an analysis of mainstream economic methodology that looks at the methods economists use in their research, and it offers some suggestions for fruitful methods in seeking knowledge about economics.

This project was started in 1983 and has been written a little at a time over a six-year period. My original plans were more modest than a book, and for several years the manuscript remained a working paper that grew a few pages at a time. Despite the warnings of a colleague not to "fall into the black hole of methodology," I continued to devote occasional periods to the project until the paper grew so unwieldly that I had to break it up into several chapters. At that time it was perhaps already too late to avoid the black hole, and completing the project appeared to be the only escape. But while the project was started several years ago, many other projects have intervened—including another book that was written from start to finish while this manuscript was in progress—so I have been practicing economic methodology as well as preaching it as I have developed the ideas in this book.

I cannot claim originality in the ideas: they all have their origins elsewhere, and I have tried to document them in the book. However, there are a great many ideas to choose from, so while the ideas may not have originated with me, I do have to take the credit or blame for the logical organization of the book as well as the choice of the ideas included and omitted, emphasized, endorsed, and criticized. I would like to be able to say that I knew everything in this book before I started to write it and that my methodological beliefs have remained unchanged as I have worked on it, but this is not true. My knowledge of methodological issues has been expanded, which is to be expected, but my own methodological views have evolved along the way as well.

I am grateful to a large number of colleagues and friends for comments and criticisms as my work has progressed. Any attempt to list them would surely leave out someone, but some of those who deserve credit for helpful comments are Don Bellante, Don Boudreaux, Steve Caudill, Bob Ekelund, Roger Garrison, Bob Hebert, Lora Holcombe, John Jackson, Roger Koppl, Steve Morell, and Leland Yeager. As this book was being written, Ross, my first child, was born, and it is to him that the book is dedicated.

Randall G. Holcombe

Economic
Models
and
Methodology

Chapter 1

INTRODUCTION

> Those who can, do science; those who can't prattle about its methodology.
>
> Paul Samuelson (1983, p. 7)

The ultimate goal of economics is to discover truths about economic relationships in the real world,[1] but there are many ways to seek the truth. Some look for empirical verification as the evidence that must support a theory before it can be accepted. Others assert that economic truths can be discovered only by logical deduction. The methods used by economists vary tremendously, but the common element that runs throughout economic analysis is the reliance on models. Economic models act as an analogy to the real world. The world is complex and difficult to understand, and the economist's model is a simplified representation it. The economist understands how the model works, and if it works analogously to a certain aspect of the real world, then the economist understands how that aspect of the real world works. The world is too complex for anyone to ever hope to understand all of its interrelationships simultaneously, but small aspects of the world can be represented by comprehensible models. Economists use models because by understanding various models of the economy, the economy that is too complex to be understood in its entirety can be understood by knowing how its component parts work and how they are interrelated.

If the object of the models is to discover truths about the world, then an important question is ask whether the conclusions of economic models can be extrapolated to the real world. Ultimately, this is an epistemological question. What is knowledge, and how does one know that one's knowledge is correct? This question is discussed briefly in this introductory chapter, but its answer really lies beyond the intended scope of this book. The object here is the more limited one of discussing what a model is, how it is developed, and how it is used in economics. In the process, the discussion will touch on both more and less preferable methods, but the book is meant as a treatise on economic practice rather than on epistemology. Since the common ground in all contemporary economic method is the use of models, an examination of the use of models seems like the ideal starting place for a methodological inquiry.

Paul Samuelson's quotation at the beginning of this chapter suggests that methodological inquiry is not really a scientific endeavor. Without debating what constitutes science, there still seems to be a benefit in examining the way in which models can be used for understanding characteristics of the real world. The book begins by looking at models in general to see how they are used to understand real world phenomena, and then the general conclusions of the first several chapters are applied to economics. Considering the use of models in economics sheds light on the way in which economists work and the way in which economic knowledge is ultimately discovered and applied. In the same way that a mechanic will be better equipped if he understands the tools at his disposal, so the economist will be better equipped by understanding his tools. Economic models are the tools of the economist.

The tool analogy is a good one because it provides some motivation for the study of methodological issues. It is not a matter of being interested in methodology for its own sake, but rather learning more about the tools of one's trade in order to do a better job. Certainly one learns about economic models just by using them in the same way that one learns about a stereo tape deck or a microwave oven by using them, but one can often become more adept at using the appliances by reading the instruction manuals. One should hope that the study of economic methodology would serve the user the same way. By gaining a fuller understanding of the way in which models work, they can be used more effectively and with fewer mistakes. This book is written in that spirit. By understanding why models work as they do, the user can apply them more effectively.

The tool analogy also sheds light on the truth in Samuelson's quotation at the beginning of the chapter. One can prattle on endlessly about the proper methods for using a hammer and saw without ever getting anything built. Methodological discussion is much like this, for it examines how one builds (or should build) in economics without ever constructing anything. One can learn much about the best building techniques by following examples of good construction, surely, and Samuelson's quotation shows that he does not consider a discourse on the use of tools to be in the same category as building something. Nevertheless, the potential value of a study in methodology is that it can illuminate builders on the nature and use of their tools. Model builders who understand their tools better can build better models. This is the potential contribution of economic methodology to economic science.

POSITIVE AND NORMATIVE METHODOLOGY

Methodological work might be thought of as falling in a continuum between two extremes. On the one extreme, positive methodology offers a description of methodology as it is. For example, Kuhn's well known treatise on methodology[2] is positive in nature, describing how scientific methodology actually works. At the other extreme is normative methodology that suggests the methodology that should be used. Of course, methodological works may have elements of each.

This book begins on a positive foundation, describing the way in which models are used generally. However, if models are the tools of the economist's trade, there are likely to be effective and ineffective ways to use them. One can drive a nail with a pipe wrench, but a hammer is more effective. The same is true of economic models. And just as an amateur carpenter could ruin a piece of wood by using the wrong tools, so could the inappropriate use of economic models lead to poor results. The reader can see where this discussion is heading: the positive discussion about the way in which models are used ultimately leads to some normative prescriptions about the way in which they should be used.

Methodological prescriptions must be used cautiously, though, because when one is seeking knowledge it is impossible to know ahead of time what method of inquiry will lead to the most insightful results. It would, therefore, seem inappropriate to brand some types of inquiry as illegitimate, or even more extreme, to claim that true knowledge cannot be found except by a particular method of inquiry.

Leaving the door open to all types of inquiry is different from claiming that one method is as good as any other, however. For one thing, some methods may have a better record of producing fruitful results than others, and this information would be useful to anyone embarking on a search for knowledge. Perhaps what is more significant is that a conclusion reached by one method might be more reliable than a conclusion reached by another. Conclusions reached by a model of the real world do not necessarily generalize to the real world, and one is likely to have more confidence in the generalizability of a model if one has confidence in the methodology used to generate the conclusions of the model.

Going beyond a simple description of economic methodology to suggesting that the conclusions reached by some methods would be more generally accepted as knowledge than conclusions reached by other methods does not seem unreasonable, and is the basis for normative methodological conclusions. Such conclusions do not mean that one methodology is right and another methodology is wrong, but rather that one can have more confidence that the results produced by one methodology represent the facts of the real world better than the results of another methodology.

EPISTEMOLOGICAL QUESTIONS

A discussion of methodology ultimately must find its roots in the epistemological questions about how one knows what one knows and how it is possible to know anything. This treatise on economic methodology will bypass the most fundamental of those questions, if only because in economics there is typically not a question about the facts that the discipline tries to explain. Thus, the facts about the real world will be taken as given throughout.

There is, perhaps, some ambiguity in the way that the word fact is being used here, so that deserves discussion. Any fact, it might be argued, is theory-laden because there must be a theory implied to allow the fact to be interpreted. For example, consider a person sitting on a chair. How would the person know that he is sitting in a chair? He can feel it under him, and he can see it. But this requires a theory to connect the sensory perceptions with phenomena in the real world.

How does one know that the implied theory connecting the sensory perceptions to the real world is correct? While this may be an interesting question, it is not especially relevant to economics because there is little disagreement on the nature of economic phenomena that are trying to be understood. All economists see the same macroeconomic fluctuations, so while these facts may be theory-laden in an epistemological sense, they are not theory-laden from an economist's perspective, since all theories tend to recognize the same real world facts. It is the causal relationships that are really subject to question.

There may be disagreement among economists over what facts one should try to explain with a theory or what real world events should be included in the theory. For example, can macroeconomic fluctuations be described solely by a theory composed of economic aggregates, like the Keynesian theory? Maybe the theory should instead be based on a foundation of individual behavior, like the monetarist and rational expectations theories. Even these theories end up looking at aggregates like the aggregate price level, aggregate employment, and so forth, whereas a business cycle theory like Hayek's[3] explicitly considers the changes in relative prices and the relative outputs and employment in particular types of industries. There are three different levels of aggregation here, and so in a sense three different sets of facts. Which one is the correct set?

This is not an epistemological question because the Keynesian theory, while it aggregates prices, employment, output, and so forth, does not deny the existence of individual prices or any of the other individual phenomena. Likewise, a Hayekian would not deny the possibility of aggregating prices, output, and so forth according to the rules of national income accounting to come up with a measure of aggregate output and a price level. The Hayekian might argue that by doing so the fundamental causes of a business cycle are eliminated from the aggregated data, but this is a question about how the data of the real world are to be used rather than a question about the fundamental facts.

For terminological clarity one might say that everything that happens in the real world is an event, but there are so many events that theories must be used to select the facts to be studied by the theorist. In economics there is little dispute that the facts of all theories are based on real world events so that a treatise on economic method can avoid considering the question of how one knows that a real world event has occurred. The methodological problem then becomes one of selecting from the universe of generally agreed-upon events some specific events to be used as the facts to be explained in a theory. In this study the facts of the real world are taken as given to concentrate on the way that economists use economic models to try to understand, explain, and predict events.

SUMMARY REMARKS

This introduction suggests the orientation of the chapters that follow. It should prevent the reader from being caught unaware of the direction in which the book is heading. Economic models are the common starting ground of economic methodology, despite divergence at that point. This enables Chapter 2 on models and their uses to begin at a point common to most economists.

From there the material narrows to examine the virtues of certain methodological devices, implying that some economics is on sounder methodological ground than others. Thus, as the book moves from analyzing the common ground of model use in economics to specific characteristics of models many readers are likely to disagree with the conclusions reached. For this reason, a forewarning is in order. Being forewarned, the reader can carefully keep track of the argument to discover at what stages his or her own views diverge from the argument in the book.

Donald McCloskey has noted that after the appearance of Milton Friedman's influential article on methodology the economics profession had largely adopted positivism as the method of economics, at least in their words if not in their deeds.[4] This made it fashionable in the profession to advocate some type of economic method; even those against positivism as a method stood ready to suggest substitutes. Recent work on methodology argues that positivism is inherently unworkable, and suggests in its place a methodological pluralism. According to pluralism, there is no single methodology that is the correct one for discovering economic truths.[5] Positivism is out, but no single method can be recommended to replace it.

Contrary to the current fashion in methodological work, this book does find certain methodological precepts to be capable of generating more fruitful results than other methods. These are not as simple or as unified as the precepts of positivism, and certainly the reader could accept some while rejecting others. Perhaps, therefore, they are better called a set of methodological principles than a methodology per se, but this is a semantic distinction. The bottom line is that the book argues that some methods are better than others. As noted earlier, this is not meant that some methods are illegitimate, but rather that one can have more confidence in the conclusions reached by some methods than the conclusions reached by others.

This being the case, the book is one not only of explanation but also of persuasion. The next two chapters deal in some detail with the way that models are used in general. They are intended as a foundation for the material to come later and they are important to the specific conclusions drawn about economic models later. With this brief introduction, the use of models can now be examined.

NOTES

1. This statement could be challenged in two directions. One is that different people might have different goals. Some people pursue economics in order to prescribe solutions to social problems, for example. The goal of the individual is to improve social conditions, but the goal of the underlying economics is to provide information about the consequences of alternative policies, so the statement stands. Some individuals might be interested in theory without regard to the real world. Chapter 4 discusses this issue, but it is reference to the real world that underlies the theory. On a deeper level, one might question whether there actually are objective truths to be discovered. This epistemological question is considered later in the chapter. Regardless of other motivations, economists are able to analyze and evaluate the work of other

economists because their theories purport to illuminate real world phenomena. In this sense, all economics attempts to discover truths about the real world.

2. Thomas S. Kuhn, *The Structure of Scientific Revolutions* (Chicago: University of Chicago Press, 1962).

3. See, for example, Friedrich A. Hayek, *Monetary Theory and the Trade Cycle* (New York: Augustus M. Kelley, 1966 [originally 1933]).

4. Donald N. McCloskey, "The Rhetoric of Economics," *Journal of Economic Literature* 21, no. 2 (June 1983), pp. 481–517, commenting on Milton Friedman, "The Methodology of Positive Economics," in *Essays in Positive Economics* (Chicago: University of Chicago Press, 1953). The same theme is present in McCloskey's *The Rhetoric of Economics* (Madison: University of Wisconsin Press, 1985).

5. See McCloskey, cited above, on this, and also Bruce J. Caldwell, *Beyond Positivism: Economic Methodology in the Twentieth Century* (London: George Allen and Unwin, 1982).

Chapter 2

MODELS AND THEIR USES

Economists, like artists, are often in love with their models.
Source unknown.

The common characteristic that pervades modern economics is the reliance on economic models as a foundation for understanding economic phenomena. Economists often find themselves in disagreement on specific issues, but without fail the basis of the disagreement is founded on the differences in the models that are being used. Perhaps the observation that economists rely on models to understand economic phenomena is obvious to the economist. If so, it provides the ideal starting point for the discussion of models, since it is a common bond that unites all economic methodology. A model is a simplified representation of its subject that provides a framework for analysis. This description naturally points to the subject of analysis, and economics analyzes economic phenomena from the real world. The goal of the modeling process is to describe as accurately as possible the phenomena being analyzed.[1] In economics, models are developed to correspond to something in the real world, leading to a natural relationship between the models and the facts of the real world. This chapter discusses economic models and methodology using as a point of departure the relationship between the model and the phenomena being modeled.

If model building is the methodological common ground of economists, the profession begins to diverge at that point, on questions ranging from how the models should be developed to how they should be applied. One extreme argues that models should be developed deductively, as a purely logical undertaking. The other extreme argues that economic phenomena can only be described by appeal to the data. All economic questions are empirical questions. In between lie those who believe that a model can be developed deductively, but empirical work can refine the model and provide additional insights. These issues will be discussed later in the book, and are not relevant to this chapter. The present chapter will consider only the role of models and the way that models are used. This discussion will then be used as a foundation for exploring how models are developed, and how they can be evaluated.

The quotation that begins the chapter implies that economic models can be beautiful creations, worthy of admiration in their own right.[2] This is certainly true, but this chapter will focus on the usefulness of a model in depicting real world phenomena. The quotation about artists and their models serves a second function as well, in pointing out the different uses of the term "model." If the term were used in art the same way it is used in economics, then in fact the artist's model would be the original—the real world of economics. The work of art is then a model of the original. It may be that the artist views the work of art as the original, and the model as a plan to work from, much as blueprints might be viewed as the architect's model from which a building is built. Sometimes, as when a portrait is being painted, the work of art is obviously intended to be a model of the original, while at other times the work of art is the original that only used the real world as a model from which to extract an inspiration.

In economics, the real world might be viewed as a model from which elegant and aesthetically pleasing representations can be developed, but in general economic models are intended to accurately portray the real world —to be a sort of portrait. One way to explore the use of models in general is to use the analogy of a map as a model. A map is intended to be a sort of portrait of the real world in that it accurately depicts certain features. Like economic models, maps are also simplifications. The analogy of maps as models will be explored in some detail, because it lends a great deal of insight into the role of models in general while eliminating any bias that an economist might have about the way that models should be developed or used.

MAPS AS MODELS

Baumol and Blinder, when introducing the concept of a model in their introductory economics book, use a map as an example.[3] Their example of a map as a model illuminates the role of models in economics, and will be used as a springboard for the discussion of this chapter. A map, in fact, is a model, and the way in which it is used helps to understand the way in which economic models are used.

Imagine that a person wished to drive from Atlanta to Los Angeles. The person not familiar with the roads between the two cities could still make the trip, probably just as efficiently as the person familiar with the route, by using a map as a guide. The map is really a model of the geographical area over which the person will be traveling. A quick look at the map will reveal that it is not a very realistic depiction of the geographical area, however. For one thing, the map is much smaller than the actual area to be covered. For another thing, many details of the area are not depicted on the map. Some towns will be missing altogether, and other towns will be depicted as small circles.

Although the map does not include some details, other details will be emphasized. Interstate highways, for example, may be shown as big blue parallel lines with numbered shields on them. The shields will be larger than many cities, and even the width of the highway will be greater than the diameter of some small circles depicting cities. This is quite unrealistic, yet it is the very unrealism of the map that makes it easier to understand the highway system that will take the traveler to Los Angeles. The important aspects of the highway system are highlighted, and the unimportant aspects are de-emphasized or left out. The driver, for example, will cross many bridges that are not shown on the map, so the map leaves out not only details outside the route of travel, but also details on the route that are deemed too inconsequential to show.

As a model for the driver, the map emphasizes the important details that the driver would have trouble seeing if every geographical detail were shown on the map. It unrealistically depicts the color and size of roads, but by doing so enhances the map reader's overall understanding of the road system. An economic model does the same thing. It makes simplifying assumptions that leave out many of the details of the real world in order to emphasize and highlight the particular economic phenomena that the model builder wishes to emphasize. In economics, as with maps, simplifying assumptions are both desirable and necessary to enhance the understanding of the phenomena being modeled.

Baumol and Blinder explain that the traveler arriving in Los Angeles will want to use a different map to navigate around the city from the map used to find the city. Once in the city, a different map will show more of the details, such as city streets, but will not depict as large an area. Once again, there is an analogy to economic models. Different models may be more appropriate depending on the degree of detail to be analyzed.

There is an obvious parallel here regarding the level of aggregation in a model. Some models in economics will represent an industry's economic activity by a simple supply and demand curve, while for other purposes the cost and demand conditions facing individual firms must be enumerated. At times, a demand curve for the firm's output may suffice, but at other times, many demands for multiple products, along with cost interdependencies, must be considered to fully understand the phenomenon being examined. The map analogy holds up well here. Often it is sufficient to represent a city simply as a dot on a map, if, for example, one is simply passing through on an interstate highway. At other times, much more detail is needed, to locate a particular address, for example. The appropriate level of aggregation depends on the intended use, and it should be noted that for some purposes too little aggregation can be just as detrimental to understanding as too much.

The map analogy can be taken a step further than the analysis of Baumol and Blinder. What if the traveler owned an airplane, and wanted to fly to Los Angeles? In this case, the appropriate map would depict different features from the road map. More airports would be shown, and in greater detail. In addition, the map would depict the altitude of the terrain and of obstructions like broadcast towers. When navigating by air, the altitude of these obstructions is important, but when driving, the map is just as helpful if it depicts the terrain as perfectly level.

The model of the Earth used when driving does not need to depict terrain height, and so may, in essence, assume the world is flat. When flying, on the other hand, such an assumption would be inappropriate, and even dangerous. Should a model of the United States show changes in elevation? The previous example makes clear that it depends on how the model will be used. Maps can be used for purposes other than navigation. Political maps show political boundaries clearly, and often show different political jurisdictions in different colors. Physical maps emphasize terrain features. Sometimes a flat map of the world may be useful, but other times a globe will be a better representation for the problem at hand. With flat maps, one will want to choose the type of projection appropriate for the map's intended use.

THE IDEAL MAP

Now consider the question: What would constitute the ideal map? Keeping in mind the above discussion, the answer would have to be that it would depend upon the use to which the map was to be put. No map is perfect for every application, and this has nothing to do with the fact that the art of mapmaking has not been perfected. A map, as a model of reality, necessarily leaves out some details in order to emphasize other details relevant to a particular problem. A map designed for one task, in order to maximize its clarity and usefulness, will be inappropriate for some other tasks. The essence of model building is that the models deliberately simplify the real world in order to focus on some particular features. An ideal map for one purpose is not the ideal map for all purposes.

The reason is that a map is a simplification that emphasizes aspects of the real world crucial to the phenomenon being examined, while ignoring other phenomena altogether. The inessential details for one application could be crucial for another. A road map does not need to contain information about the height of radio towers or mountain peaks, or the location of most airports. To include them on a road map, while it would make the map more realistic, would also reduce the clarity of the map and make it more difficult to understand how to drive from one location to another. The key element to any model is that the model is deliberately unrealistic, and is unrealistically simple. It leaves out nonessential elements to allow the user to focus on the features of the real world that are important to the particular phenomenon under study.

To say that a model is unrealistic or simple is never a criticism, it is just a description of all models. Of course, a model may be inappropriate to the matter under study, but this is a different problem altogether. Simplification and unrealism are the characteristics of models.

This discussion has attempted to draw a parallel between maps as models of the physical world and economic models as models of economic phenomena. All of the points made regarding the relationships between maps and the real world also apply to economic models and the real world. The map analogy can help to clarify some aspects of economic model building because maps are, in fact, models of the real world.

TYPES OF ASSUMPTIONS

The above discussion indicates that assumptions are necessary in models to make the models understandable depictions of reality. All assumptions are not used in the same way, however, and in an insightful discussion, Alan Musgrave has divided assumptions into three distinct categories.[4] One category is the negligibility assumption. In this case, the impact of some phenomena is so small that the benefits of including the phenomena in the model are outweighed by the cost of additional complexity in the model, making the model, overall, more difficult to understand. An example from economics is the assuming away of income effects, or the assumption of lump sum taxes.[5] A second type of assumption is the domain assumption, which states that the model can be expected to accurately depict reality as long as certain conditions exist (or do not exist, as the assumption specifies). The third type of assumption is what Musgrave labels a heuristic assumption.[6] This type of assumption models something as definitely different from the way it is in the real world, but under the supposition that the unrealism of the assumption will not affect the result.[7]

An example of a heuristic assumption from the map analogy occurs when highways on the map are depicted as red and blue lines, even though no highways are actually those colors. However, this depiction makes it easier to use the map to travel, as long as the color of the road is not crucial. Similarly, in economics, sometimes industries are assumed to be competitive even though they have some ability to set the prices of their output. There are several reasons why simplifying assumptions of all types may be used, and different simplifying assumptions may have different purposes.

A bit more should be said here regarding heuristic assumptions, particularly since the term is used in a slightly different way by Alan Musgrave. The similarity in the way Musgrave uses the term and the way it is used here is that in both cases a heuristic assumption is an assumption that is obviously unrealistic. The use of a heuristic assumption, as Musgrave explains it, is to illustrate a counterfactual situation. For example, an economist may assume an industry to be perfectly competitive even when it obviously is not in order to contrast that situation with the actual situation in the market, and to clearly illustrate the effects of the actual situation involving less than perfect competition. The economist will recognize that this use of heuristic assumptions appears frequently in economic analysis.

Heuristic assumptions may also be used in another way. An industry may be assumed to be perfectly competitive when it is not because for the purpose at hand, the lack of perfect competition does not affect the conclusion of the model. Thus, when looking at the particular industry, it could be modeled as perfectly competitive for some purposes, but not for others. This use of heuristic assumptions is also common in economics, and is directly suggested in the map analogy. After all, roads are not red and blue lines in reality, but the very unrealism of this aspect of the model makes it easier to understand and use the model to get from one point to another.

Similar assumptions in economics eliminate complicated details by assuming a simpler state of the world when the more complex state would yield the same conclusions. Frequently, economists will assume all firms to be the same size, taxes to be lump-sum, or transactions costs to be zero. These types of heuristic assumptions are sometimes made to compare the actual state of the world with some other imaginary state of the world, but frequently they are also made along with the modeler's claim that the results lose no generality because of the simplifying assumptions. Returning to the map analogy, certainly the ability to arrive at one's destination is enhanced by many unrealistic features on the map.

Musgrave might want to put this use of a heuristic assumption into the negligibility category instead. The color of the road has a negligible effect on the outcome of the trip. There is no need to engage in terminological debates, but some distinctions can be made here. Normally, something will be assumed away if it is negligible, but a heuristic device may assume it to be different from how it is in the real world as a way to facilitate understanding, if the difference in the assumption does not affect the outcome. One is not assuming that there are no roads, or that their color is unimportant. To the contrary, interstate highways are represented as blue lines on the map to identify them, even though this heuristic assumption is contrary to fact. Modeling interstate highways as blue makes it easier to understand how to make the trip, but does not alter the route to be taken.

Musgrave's taxonomy of assumptions helps to clarify the different roles that assumptions play in the construction of models. This taxonomy will be drawn upon later in the book, so it is important at this point to see the distinction among the types. With negligibility assumptions, the assumption is made because the factor assumed to be negligible will have little effect on the outcome in the real world. With domain assumptions, the model is asserted to be an accurate depiction of reality only within the assumed domain. With heuristic assumptions, a deliberately unrealistic assumption is made to enhance the understanding of the model.

In closing this section, the map analogy can be used to consider some of the distinctions between negligibility assumptions and heuristic assumptions. Heuristic assumptions may be used to examine counterfactual situations, but more interesting for purposes of comparison is the situation where a heuristic assumption is employed as a simplifying assumption because it is alleged not to change the outcome of a model. For example, the road map does not depict changes in elevation as a simplifying assumption about the real world. Changes in elevation will have a negligible effect on the driver's navigation, even though the effects could be significant in some circumstances. Someone with heart problems may want to avoid high altitudes, and someone towing a heavy trailer may want to avoid steep grades. Nevertheless, most road maps depict the earth as flat because changes in altitude will have a negligible effect on a trip. This is a negligibility assumption.

Contrast this with the situation where roads are displayed as red and blue lines, or where different countries are displayed in different colors. In these cases, the colors are heuristic devices intended to enhance the understanding of a particular aspect of the world by depicting some of its characteristics in a purposefully unrealistic manner. Political boundaries can be better understood if different countries are depicted as different colors, even though in reality this is not the case. Likewise, the routing of interstate highways can be better understood if they are shown as parallel blue lines, even though their true color is not blue. This point deserves some emphasis because of the way that heuristic assumptions are frequently used in economics.

With regard to the maps, one would not be able to distinguish passing from one political jurisdiction to another by examining the color of the earth as one traveled. Likewise, one would not succeed in finding an interstate highway by searching for a blue road. The analogy holds in economic models as well. Some assumptions could be applied to a model for some purposes that would be totally inappropriate in others. For example, a model that assumes perfect competition in an industry cannot be dismissed out-of-hand if the industry is shown to be oligopolistic. The assumption of competition may clarify some aspects of the industry's economic behavior, even though it may be totally inappropriate in other instances. Heuristic assumptions must be judged within the context that they are used.

This is not an argument in favor of methodological positivism, as will be made clear in the chapter on positivism. The appropriateness of heuristic assumptions can—and should—be judged on grounds beyond the model's ability to predict. But here, the argument is getting ahead of itself, and additional discussion will be deferred to the chapter discussing positivism.

ECONOMIC MODELS

Economic models are designed for the purpose of depicting the essential aspects of some economic phenomena. Many details of the real world will necessarily be left out of any economic model, because it is simply not possible to take account of everything. To do so would produce a model as complex as the real world, and presumably the reason the model was constructed in the first place was that the real world was too complex to understand by itself, outside the framework of a model. Thus, the fact that a model abstracts from some aspects of reality, while necessary, is also a virtue, because it is an aid to understanding the process being modeled. By abstracting from the complications that are only of secondary importance, the economic model focuses its attention on the most important economic factors.

A direct consequence of this is that no single economic model will ever be appropriate for analyzing all economic phenomena. The very nature of a model precludes this. A model abstracts from some features of reality, and so cannot possibly model all aspects of reality. For example, the current economic paradigm[8] relies on the notion of equilibrium for an understanding of the state toward which economic forces pull the economy. This is the case despite the diverse and sometimes contradictory models of equilibrium to which economists refer. Equilibrium might refer to Walrasian general equilibrium, a Keynesian IS-LM equilibrium, a Marshallian partial equilibrium, or the evenly rotating economy described by Mises.[9]

By abstracting from many elements of economic activity, these models of equilibrium provide insight into the way an economy operates. As a result of their simplicity, however, they are inappropriate for analyzing some economic phenomena. None of the equilibrium models just mentioned can explain how the economy moves from one equilibrium position to another, for example. The forces of adjustment from one equilibrium to another lie outside the model.

The economist who is questioned about how the economy moves from one equilibrium to another will typically describe the equilibrating process in another model where individuals trade in response to present incentives and expectations about the future. Typically, this equilibrating model is richer in institutional detail than the equilibrium model, but in any event, it is different. Often, equilibrating models never reach equilibrium. Neoclassical models of search and information move toward equilibrium, but never arrive at the equilibrium state described by neoclassical economics. Austrian models of entrepreneurship[10] contain an equilibrating process, but never arrive at the evenly rotating economy. Models of the adjustment process in general do not arrive at an equilibrium, and equilibrium models in general do not contain an adjustment process.

The details of particular models are not at issue here. Rather, there is a general question about the use of economic models that are inconsistent, perhaps in their assumptions, perhaps in their details, and perhaps in their conclusions. If the map analogy applies, the answer is that the appropriate model depends upon the use to which the model will be put. When trying to analyze the likely effects of an oil import quota on the price of gasoline, it may be acceptable (and desirable, for the sake of simplicity) to model the industry as perfectly competitive. When trying to explain the different prices and market shares of various retailers of gasoline, the perfectly competitive assumption will be inappropriate. Again, the point is that different models will be appropriate for different purposes.

To summarize, economic models are simplified analytical frameworks for depicting particular economic phenomena. The simplification is both necessary and desirable. A model with no simplification would be as complex as the real world, and as difficult to understand. By using a model, aspects that are unimportant to the phenomenon being studied can be abstracted, allowing attention to be focused on the important relationships of the problem under study. Because of the nature of a model, no one economic model can hope to describe all economic activity. The appropriate model depends upon the problem to which it will be applied. The best model for one purpose will be inappropriate for some others. This being the case, one task that faces the analyst is selecting the appropriate model for the problem at hand. Much of the remainder of the book deals with this problem.

CONCLUSION

This chapter is intended to serve as a general introduction to the concept of models, and the way models are used to represent the real world. The chapter has relied heavily on the example of a map as a model in order to make some general points without slipping too heavily into areas where economists might have methodological preconceptions about how economic models ought to be used. The map serves as a good example, because a map is in fact a model, and one that has obvious and straightforward uses familiar to everyone. This should help to clarify the role of models in economics, where the usefulness of some models is not always so obvious. If the reader considers the arguments in this chapter to be obvious—to be things that everyone already knows—then it has served its purpose as a good introduction to the material that follows. The later chapters that consider the use of models by economists are all built upon the general concepts on the use of models presented here.

The map analogy employed throughout the chapter led to several conclusions regarding the way models are used, and the reason for using models at all. The reason why models are used is because the real world is a very complex place, and to understand particular real-world phenomena, many of the details of the real world must be omitted from examination. This is a necessity. The real world is so complex that all of its nuances can never be comprehended all at once. A model is a framework for analysis that considers only some aspects of the real world, and thus makes it easier to understand the particular real-world phenomena being modeled.

Several lessons can be drawn directly from the map analogy in the chapter. First, models are deliberately unrealistic. Some features are omitted altogether, while some features are grossly exaggerated. The reason for this is to accentuate the important aspects of the phenomena being modeled. Some of the unrealism comes from assumptions of negligibility. Features are left out of the model if their impact on the model's conclusion will be negligible. Some unrealism comes from heuristic assumptions. A heuristic assumption depicts the world as different from the way it is in reality. For example, a country may be shown on a map as being a red color when the true country is not red, or an industry can be depicted in an economic model as being competitive when in fact the firms in the industry have some power to set their own prices. Heuristic assumptions can be useful to emphasize features important to the phenomena under examination, even if the assumption would be misleading under some circumstances. The political map showing the red country does so in order to accentuate political boundaries, and aids in understanding in this context, even though it is not realistic. Likewise, the assumption of perfect competition in the oil industry may add clarity to a model explaining the effects of a tariff on imported oil, but it would be an inappropriate assumption in a model trying to explain the pricing structure in the industry. Thus, the appropriateness of an assumption in a model cannot be judged independently of the use to which the model is to be put.

Since a model is, of necessity, a simplified view of the world, it stands to reason that a single model cannot hope to explain all of the complexities of the world. Different models will be appropriate for different purposes. Assumptions that simplify a model for one purpose may eliminate some of the crucial aspects of reality for another. Sometimes the differences will have to do with scale and detail. For example, a map of the United States would be inappropriate for finding a particular street address in Atlanta. Likewise, a complex general equilibrium model may not be appropriate for examining the impact of zoning regulations on property values in a particular area. In both cases, the larger scale models contain many aspects that are of minor importance to the task at hand, but leave out some important details relevant to the current question.

Questions of scale are not the only relevant differences in models. One would use a different map of the United States to cross the country by air as opposed to driving across. Likewise, a comparative statics model might be appropriate for understanding the structure of equilibrium prices in an industry, but cannot show the dynamics of price change. The point is that because models necessarily abstract from some elements of reality, no model can accurately depict every real-world phenomenon. Elements assumed away in one model may be important factors in some real-world occurrences. This is not a drawback of the model, but a necessary characteristic of all models. Models simplify reality in order to accentuate the important aspects of reality, while ignoring others. Factors important to some phenomena will be insignificant in others.

What constitutes the perfect model? This depends on the use to which the model is to be put. A model appropriate for some uses will be inappropriate for others. For any particular purpose, a good model will accentuate the important causes and effects, while ignoring those that are not important. The appropriate model is the one that includes the important aspects for the application at hand. This much said, the next question is how to find the appropriate model. Discussion of this question will be deferred until later chapters, but the theme of this chapter suggests that all models are not equally appropriate.[11] Before discussing issues of model selection, the next chapter deals with some details on the nature of models and their development.

NOTES

1. This leaves open the question about how the accuracy of the description is assessed. A methodological positivist, for example, might use predictive ability as the measuring rod. This issue will be considered in depth later.

2. A similar quotation appears in Edward E. Leamer, "Let's Take the Con Out of Econometrics," *American Economic Review* 73, no. 1 (1983), pp. 31–43, who also cites the author as anonymous.

3. William J. Baumol and Alan S. Blinder, *Economics: Principles and Policy*, 2d ed. (New York: Harcourt Brace Jovanovich, Inc., 1982), pp. 10–13. James M. Buchanan, "What Should Economists Do?" *Southern Economic Journal* 30, no. 3 (January 1964), pp. 213–22, uses a map analogy as well, but in a slightly different context.

4. Alan Musgrave, " 'Unreal' Assumptions in Economic Theory," *Kyklos* 34. Fasc. 3 (1981), pp. 377–87. The taxonomy described here deviates to some degree from Musgrave's article, although his discussion is quite illuminating and appropriate to assumptions in economic models generally.

5. Kevin D. Hoover, "Two Types of Monetarism," *Journal of Economic Literature* 22, no. 1 (March 1984), pp. 58–76, has a very illuminating discussion on this subject, relating partial equilibrium analysis to general equilibrium analysis.

6. The present use of the term is similar to Musgrave's use, but is not identical.

7. The Greek root of heuristic means to invent or discover, and the English word refers to a method of education in which students are taught to find out things for themselves. Presumably, then, the heuristic assumption helps the model's users to understand about the world despite the assumption's unrealism.

8. The term here is being used in the same sense as in Thomas S. Kuhn, *The Structure of Scientific Revolutions* (Chicago: University of Chicago Press, 1962).

9. Hoover's "Two Kinds of Monetarism," referenced earlier, provides an illuminating discussion of the distinction between partial equilibrium and general equilibrium models.

10. The model of Israel M. Kirzner, *Competition and Entrepreneurship* (Chicago: University of Chicago Press, 1973) is an example.

11. Thus, the eclectic approach endorsed by Bruce J. Caldwell, *Beyond Positivism: Economic Methodology in the Twentieth Century* (London: George Allen and Unwin, 1982) will not be endorsed here.

Chapter 3

MODELS, THEORIES, AND DATA

A Theory is the way we perceive "facts," and we cannot perceive "facts" without a theory.

Milton Friedman (1953, p. 34).

The previous chapter explained how and why models are used. This chapter will discuss how they are developed. Models can be developed in two different ways: from theories, and from data. In economics, models and theories have a relationship so close that the distinction deserves some discussion, and the first part of the chapter is devoted to discussing the relationships among models, theories, and data. Economic models, as they are typically presented by economists, are developed deductively. It will be argued, however, that inductive reasoning plays a crucial role in the development of economic knowledge, and that in economics, every model has a significant inductive foundation, derived from empirical observation. Chapter 4 looks into the roles of inductive and deductive reasoning in economics in more detail. The present chapter is more concerned with the way models are developed, the way that axioms and assumptions are used in economics, and the ultimate uses of models.

The first part of the chapter on the relationships among models, theories, and data is general, and applies to scientific inquiry in general. The next section, discussing deductive versus inductive reasoning, starts from a general foundation, but applies more specifically to economics and the social sciences because of the differences in the subject matter and the data available to social scientists. These sections are followed by a section on economics as an empirical science. There, it is argued that economics, because of its subject matter, is fundamentally an empirical science. This argument is then followed by a discussion on the uses of axioms and assumptions in economics. This material logically follows the previous chapter on models and their uses by discussing the development of models, and also serves as a transition from the discussion of models in general to the specific uses of models in economics.

THEORIES

A theory is a coherent group of general propositions used as principles of explanation for a general class of phenomena. Theories by themselves do not explain real-world phenomena, but must be incorporated into models. Einstein's theory of relativity does not say anything about the real world, nor does the theory of consumer behavior. However, armed with the theory, logical deduction can lead to the development of a model that says that if some initial conditions are met, then some conclusions about the real world can be drawn. Note that the reason that a theory does not say anything about the real world directly is because assumptions about the real world are needed to make the theory conform to the real world.

For example, a theory might specify that in a vacuum, the Earth's gravity will cause falling bodies to accelerate at 32 feet per second per second. This means that if a two-ton automobile were dropped from the same height as a sixteen-pound shot put, they both should hit the ground at the same time. The reader willing to try this experiment will find the theory confirmed. This also means that if a two-ton automobile were dropped from the same height as a feather, both should hit the ground at the same time. The reader willing to try this experiment will find that the automobile hits the ground first.

Two lessons can be drawn from this. First, for objects with relatively small surface areas compared to their masses, like automobiles and shot puts, the effects of air resistance can safely be assumed away. In other words, a vacuum can be assumed as a negligibility assumption, to use the terminology from the previous chapter. The assumption is unwarranted with regard to the feather, however. As was noted in the previous chapter, simplifying assumptions that are warranted in some situations may be inappropriate in others.

The second thing to note is that the theory itself says nothing about the real world. If the shot put and automobile experiment is viewed as a confirmation of the theory, then the feather and automobile experiment must be viewed as contradicting the theory. In fact, the theory must be accompanied by assumptions about the real world, and what is being tested is a combination of the theory and the assumptions. The planets Neptune and Pluto were both discovered because the other outer planets were not moving exactly as predicted theoretically. The anomalous movements were not taken as a refutation of the theory, but instead were taken as an indication that all of the assumptions of the theory were not being met. This happens frequently in economics as well. Evidence that seems to contradict a theory will be taken by the theory's supporters as an indication that the assumptions about the real world were not met rather than as an indication of a faulty theory. How the evidence should be taken will be discussed later in the book. At this point, it is sufficient to note that a theory by itself says nothing about the real world.[1]

Mark Blaug notes that it is difficult to even define the term theory when it is being used in a technical sense.[2] For present purposes, a theory is a hypothesis that is believed to be true. A hypothesis, in turn, is an assumption that is made to test its logical or empirical consequences.[3] Thus, a scientist may make a hypothesis, supposing the real world to be a certain way in order to test the consequences of the hypothesis. Frequently, hypotheses may be made as heuristic devices, with full knowledge that they are not true. A hypothesis believed to be true attains the status of a theory, and is in general not subject to test, in the sense noted above. Theories may be said to be tested, but typically a failed test will cause the supporting assumptions to be questioned rather than the theory. Once elevated from the status of a hypothesis, a theory is a general proposition used as a principle of explanation for a general class of phenomena.[4]

MODELS AND DATA

A model is a framework for analysis that duplicates some characteristics of the phenomena being modeled. One way to develop a model, as just noted, is to logically deduce one from a combination of theories and assumptions about the characteristics of the real world. Another way is by appeal to data. The term data as used here will simply refer to facts about the real world, whether or not they can be readily quantified. One might observe data, and from that develop a model without an underlying theory.

For example, one might observe that the weather on one day tends to be similar to the day before, which leads to a model predicting today's weather as the same as yesterday's. The model predicts all weather phenomena fairly well, from precipitation to cloud cover to temperature. This model will be called model 1. More data could lead to a better model that describes today's weather at point A as the same as yesterday's weather at point B, where point B is 200 miles to the west of A. This model predicts better, and will be called model 2. A third model could be developed that observes wind direction and speed, and computes point B in model 2 as a function of the wind. More complex weather models could be developed, but for this discussion, these three will suffice.

In this example, model 1 was developed entirely from examination of the data, and observing the strong correlation between weather on one day and the weather on the succeeding day. The model was not developed by logical deduction, and in fact the model contains a logical inconsistency. A logical implication of the model that describes today's weather as being the same as yesterday's is that the weather will never change, yet the data show the weather to change. Note that this model, even with the logical problem, may predict better than a logically consistent model. For example, the weather may be modeled as resulting from the actions of gods, such as the rain god, the wind god, and so forth. While not common today, this model of weather gods has been held by many people in the past. It offers the logical benefit of allowing for change, although its predictive accuracy may be less than the logically inconsistent model.

Which is the better model, model 1 or the model where the weather gods control the weather? If the choices are limited to those two, the logical positivist would select model 1, while an individual believing that models of the real world had to satisfy the criterion of logical consistency would select the weather gods model. However, if model 1 has greater predictive content, there is good reason for the student of weather to examine it despite its logical problem, because the predictive ability of the model suggests that may have captured some important aspect of reality.

A search through the data would discover a higher correlation between today's weather here and yesterday's weather 200 miles to the west, which could lead on empirical grounds to the development of model 2. Simply searching through the data could develop model 2 without any logical foundation, although a logical question about the reason for serial correlation in weather might suggest the answer as well. Weather systems tend to move with the prevailing westerly winds. Once the connection between wind and weather is developed, this opens the road for model 3, where wind is explicitly taken into account.

The point of this section is simply to develop the relationship among theories, models, and data. From this discussion, it should be apparent that models can exist without theories, generated entirely by the data. Road maps are models of this type, and empirical models linking cancer to some chemicals are of this type as well. It would be possible to generate economic models without theories as well. For example, a business cycle could be modeled as the sum of sine waves of various magnitudes and periods.

This example of an economic model without a theory illustrates the point, but it probably will not find ready acceptance with most economists. The reason is that in contemporary economic analysis, a model is viewed as unacceptable without a theory to support it. Thus, in economics, theories are often difficult to distinguish from the models in which they are embedded. This is simply a characteristic of the discipline of economics: contemporary economists will reject any economic model that does not have a theory to support it. The typical economic model is closely linked to a theory, so sometimes the distinction between the model and the theory is not clear. For example, the quotation by Milton Friedman at the beginning of the chapter indicates that Friedman is using the word theory to mean what is here referred to as a model. Nevertheless, models and theories are distinctly different things. A model of an economic process (for example, that the change in stock market prices is correlated with the change in hemlines) is not necessarily backed by a theory.

It is perhaps worthwhile to remark that other disciplines routinely accept models without theories. In physics, mathematical models of physical properties are completely acceptable without theories to explain them, even though models can provide a basis for seeking a theoretical explanation. Gravity is a good example. There is no theory to explain why gravity exists. Despite the fact that its cause is not understood, it is readily accepted as an empirical regularity. In medicine, statistical models without theoretical foundations are often used, and the finding that two phenomena are correlated will lead to the presumption of causation without any theoretical foundation. Cancer-causing agents are often identified this way.

Models can be developed in two ways, then. First, a theory can be buttressed by assumptions about the real world in order to make a model. Thus, the model comes from the theory. In economics, virtually all models are supported by theories, so that any economic analysis will contain a theoretical model, making the economic theory and the economic model virtually indistinguishable. The second way to develop a model is by appeal to the data. An empirical regularity is found that then acts as a model of the real world. The Phillips curve might be viewed as an economic example of this. The empirical regularity was discovered which produced the model. Since economists are reluctant to accept empirical models with no theoretical foundation, an elaborate theoretical model was developed around the empirical regularity, but it is certainly possible for the empirical model to predate the theoretical foundation. It should be remembered that in other disciplines, empirical models with no theoretical foundations are routinely accepted.

With regard to empirical models, one might well wonder if there must not be some theory lurking behind every model. An empirical model will relate real-world phenomena together, but since the real world is so complex, surely a researcher must have some theory in mind when relating data to each other. This is possible, of course, but a researcher may just use the most easily available data, or (more likely) find one empirical relationship while looking for something else. This reasoning really obscures the true relationship among models, theories, and data, however. Certainly a model can come from a theory, and economic models are typically presented as being derived from theories. However, all models and theories must ultimately have their origin in the data of the real world. The subject matter of economics lies in the real world, so there will always be a correspondence between economic models and real world data. The model is intended to correspond to the data. Economics is, at its foundation, an empirical science.

It is not possible to develop knowledge about the real world without first observing some real-world empirical regularity. This amounts to saying that the development of economic models is an inductive rather than a deductive process. Some questions regarding induction versus deduction will be taken up in the next chapter. Meanwhile, the next section lays a foundation for the discussion of induction versus deduction by examining the relationship between economic theories and the real world.

ECONOMICS AS AN EMPIRICAL SCIENCE

Economic models correspond to real-world phenomena, but, given the relationships among theories, models, and data, it is legitimate to ask whether the discovery of the phenomena led to the development of a model, or whether the development of a theory led to the development of a model and then to the discovery of the phenomena. As just noted, the process can go both ways, and instances of each case can be cited. The Phillips curve, discussed earlier, is an example of an empirical phenomenon that was discovered first. The initial model was generated by the data, and was presented as an empirical regularity. A theoretical foundation was then developed that was consistent with the empirical model. The original Keynesian theory of the Phillips curve had its critics, but it takes a theory to beat a theory, and the critics successfully developed another theory (with differing policy implications). Note, though, that even the competing theory (of the vertical long-run Phillips curve) was generated from the data, in the sense that it had to encompass the observed data that was already explained by one theory.

There is a parallel here with the weather example discussed above. The Phillips curve was discovered as an empirical phenomenon, like the weather model 1, and was linked to the

Keynesian paradigm logically to produce a theoretical model. The empirical regularity noted by Phillips in his original article was generalized to apply not only to wages and unemployment, but to price indexes in general and unemployment. The generalization should not be surprising, since different price indexes tend to be correlated with one another, but the Phillips curve model originally developed, like the weather model 1, was generalized into a second model, like weather model 2, that provided a more general understanding of the phenomenon, and led to a theory with better predictive ability. Additional theory, coupled with additional empirical evidence, led to a third model, like the weather model 3 above, in which the observed trade-off between inflation and unemployment is a short-run phenomenon. Clearly, economic models and theories can be developed beginning with the data.

The accepted methodology in economics, however, claims to do the opposite; that is, to generate empirically refutable claims about the real world that are logically deduced from theories.[5] The theory comes first, then the data are examined to see if they correspond to the theory. This method of inquiry is undeniably possible, and certainly it is a legitimate part of economic inquiry to discover logical implications of economic theories, and to see if phenomena in the real world correspond to the implications of the theory.

Where did the theory originate? It may have been deduced from another theory, but that just pushes the question one step further back, to seeking the origin of the original theory. There are two possibilities. The theory may have developed from some irrefutable logical proposition(s), or it may have come from the development of a model from some empirical phenomenon. In economics, the latter is the case. Some axioms about human behavior are posited as true, and then economic theories develop the logical implications of these axioms. The axioms themselves come from observation of human behavior in the real world, so the axioms—and the theories built on them—are ultimately empirically derived.[6] Economics is, at its foundation, an empirical science.

Human behavior is the ultimate object of the economist's study, so any initial axioms from which theorizing must start will be based on observed human behavior. From here, theories will be able to be logically deduced, but with the empirical foundation of observed behavior. From these initial axioms, it might be desirable to deduce the rest of economic theory, but in practice, theories in general—the Phillips curve is a good specific example—come from empirical observation rather than logical deduction.

To recapitulate briefly, axioms in economics are posited as a result of the observation of human behavior. Theories may be developed, using logical deduction, based on the axioms. These theories may be developed into models by making assumptions that link the conditions of the theory to the conditions of the real world. Models may also be developed by observing the real world and describing some observed empirical relationship. In economics, theories are almost always generated by empirical observation rather than by logical deduction.

This does not deny the value of logically deducing theories, even after they have been hypothesized. Once a hypothesis has been made as a result of empirical observation, it is valuable to try to logically deduce the theory from generally accepted axioms in economics. The insight that developed the theory may have been empirical, but a logical derivation of the theory, although after the fact, is important because it enables the theory to be placed within a body of other economic theories. The assumptions about the real world that are necessary for the theory to be true can be discerned, thus shedding some light on the generality of the theory. In addition, further logical deductions may lead to additional insights, or discover some other theories or phenomena inconsistent with the posited theory. Theories in general have an empirical origin, but this does not lessen the importance of being able to logically deduce the theory after the fact from generally acceptable axioms of economics.[7]

In economics, virtually all models are also theories, and the terms can be used interchangeably most times. Models with no theoretical foundation can be imagined, such as one showing the relationship between the direction of change in hemlines and the direction of change in the stock market, or the relationship between economic activity and sunspots,[8] but in general, economists develop models with underlying theories, even if the relationship being modeled was originally discovered empirically. The distinction is there, and has been useful in evaluating the origins of theories, but in economics, models have theoretical foundations.

The reason for this has to do with the subject matter of economics. Models are simplifications of the real world, and so the conclusions of a model are dependent upon the caveat that things outside the model do not affect the model's conclusions. In other words, all other things are held constant. In some areas, like engineering and physics, it is much easier to tell when all other things remain constant, and in those areas practitioners are comfortable using empirical regularities in models that do not have a theoretical foundation that is well understood. In economics, by contrast, it is not always easy to tell when other things remain constant, so a theoretical foundation is demanded by economists in order to plainly lay out to the model's users what conditions must exist for the model to be valid. This is why economists find models without theoretical foundations to be generally unacceptable.

Economic models are used to understand economic phenomena. They are helpful because the model corresponds to some real-world situation, but it is much simpler, so it is easier to understand. An economic model is an analogy which says that the world operates like the model. The amount of detail in the model will depend upon the axioms and assumptions that are used. Since the model is intended as an analogy to some real-world situation, the axioms and assumptions will come from empirical observation of the real world.

AXIOMS AND ASSUMPTIONS

Axioms in a model are propositions that are used as conventions or hypotheses. They are taken as given and are not subject to dispute. Assumptions are conditions about the real world that the model depicts as true. Axioms and assumptions have equivalent functions in economic models, since conditions assumed or taken as axiomatic are taken as given by the model. However, there is a difference in principle. Axioms in economic models are generally considered to be self-evident propositions,[9] and are not subject to dispute. The implication is that an axiom used in one model ought to be appropriate for any model, since it represents a self-evident truth about the economic behavior of individuals. Assumptions, on the other hand, may be made in an attempt to test their validity in a particular model, or, as discussed in the previous chapter, may be made heuristically, even though they are known to be false.

The previous chapter argued that the appropriate model would depend on its intended purpose. A given theory could be embodied into a model in a variety of ways. The selection of axioms and assumptions defines a model, and there are many possible starting places. For example, a very general economic framework is set up by Mises, who views utility maximization as axiomatic. A person acts only in order to make himself better off, so, axiomatically, any action is utility maximizing. This is the empirical observation that begins Mises's theory of human action. The theory is very general, and so is consistent with any behavior of the individual. The theory does not predict anything, but it describes everything.[10] Chapter 9 discusses Mises's theory of utility in more detail.

Frequently, economists employ more restrictive assumptions than those used by Mises. Neoclassical micro theorists, for example, frequently assume individuals to be maximizing their money wealth. Certainly, some real-world behavior can be observed that does not correspond with this assumption, but by restricting the possible real-world implications of the theory, the theory has more predictive content than one that takes utility maximization as axiomatic. Restrictive assumptions enhance the predictive content of a model by limiting the outcomes in the real world that would be consistent with the model. Note the difference between the axiomatic assumption of utility maximization and the assumption of wealth maximization. The axiomatic assumption of Mises is presented as a self-evident principle of human action which could never be refuted, as opposed to the wealth maximization assumption that is not presented as axiomatic. It is conceptually refutable and is used in order to enhance the predictive content of the theory.

This discussion makes restrictive assumptions appear to be a homogeneous lot, at least in a sense. The more restrictive the assumptions, the more predictive content will be embodied in the resulting theory. This is true, but all assumptions are not created equal. The relative merit of different types of assumptions will be discussed at length in later chapters, but for now, the discussion will be brief. The point to be made here is that assumptions regarding the types of choices that individuals are likely to make are far superior to assumptions that lump individuals together into behavioral aggregates. There is a separate chapter devoted to this concept of methodological individualism later in the book, so further discussion can be deferred. If the argument for methodological individualism is to be accepted, however, then it will also be the case that a model can be judged in part on the assumptions that it uses, as opposed to the positivist view that the sole criterion of the model should be its ability to predict. There is also a separate chapter devoted to methodological positivism, so discussion on this point can be deferred as well. The argument will be developed, however, that some assumptions are better than others.

Thus far this chapter has focused on the development of economic models. The next section considers the question of how economists use the models they develop.

THE USES OF ECONOMIC MODELS

Unless a model is to be considered on the basis of its intrinsic elegance or beauty, the suitability of a model for its intended purpose must be an important measure of its worth. It has already been emphasized that different models will be suitable for different purposes. Within a positive framework, there are three distinct uses for economic models. First, they can be used for prediction. This application is straightforward; a model used for this purpose implies that if event A happens, then event B will happen as a result of the occurrence of A. While it is easy to see how an existing model could be used for prediction, it is not so straightforward to establish criteria for determining the ability of an existing model to predict future events.

The second use for an economic model is to describe and organize observed phenomena. The model acts as an analogy to some real-world phenomena, but since the model is simpler than the real-world, understanding the model helps the observer to understand the essence of the real-world phenomena.

The third use of a model is to logically deduce the existence of phenomena that have not been observed. That these phenomena had not been observed could be due to three reasons. First, nobody may have looked for a phenomenon before the model alerted people to its possible existence. Second, existing techniques may not have the ability to see the phenomenon. Third, the phenomenon may be unobservable in principle.

The three roles of a model—as a predictor, an explainer, and a revealer—are closely related. An important theme that will be built upon as the book progresses is that the model as an explainer is really the foundation upon which the other uses of economic models are built. A model that cannot do a credible job as an explainer of real-world phenomena cannot be relied upon for its predictions, no matter how well it may have been able to predict in the past, and cannot be relied upon to logically deduce characteristics of the real world that have yet to be observed. If this argument is not self-evident to the reader, the discussion in later chapters will try to make it so.

A model is really an analogy to the real world. The elements in the model are not analogous to the elements in the real world; rather, the relationships among the elements of the model are analogous to the relationships among the elements in the real world.[11] It is because of the analogous relationships between the model and real world that the model is useful as a device for understanding how the real world works.[12]

CONCLUSION

Looking at the relationships among models, theories, and data, any knowledge about the real world must originally come from the observation of some characteristics of real-world phenomena. This is why the chapter argues that economics is at its foundation an empirical science. In contemporary economics, however, models without theories are not acceptable, so any economic model must be developed upon a theoretical foundation, even if the theory is developed after the fact to support some empirical observation. This is because in economics, unlike the so-called hard sciences,[13] real-world events are very complex, and it is difficult to ascertain what empirical factors are causal without a theory to explain observed phenomena. Thus, for example, a model of a business cycle as the sum of various sine waves would not be acceptable in contemporary economics without a theory to explain why the cycle behaved in this manner.

The hypothesis is the beginning of theoretical development. A hypothesis is made in order to examine its logical or empirical implications. A theory is a hypothesis that is believed to be true. A theory by itself says nothing about the real world, but must be supported by assumptions about the real world in order to describe real-world phenomena. A theory, supported by these types of assumptions, is a theoretical model. In economics, the terms theory and model are used almost interchangeably, despite the distinction. This occurs because every model has a theoretical foundation, but one must realize that when the theory is applied to the real world, as, for example, in an empirical test, it is the model that is tested, not the theory. In general, when a test result is negative, the assumptions of the model are rejected as invalid, rather than the theory itself.

Assumptions that are included in a model are of two varieties. Some are axioms, which are assumptions about the real world that are taken as self-evident, and are not open to dispute. Other assumptions describe real world characteristics that may or may not be present, and themselves fall into several categories. Assumptions can be negligibility assumptions, domain assumptions, or heuristic assumptions, as described in the previous chapter. Each type plays a different role in a model. Axioms are assumptions, but are a particular type of domain assumption, since the argument is not only that the model holds in the assumed domain, but that the assumed domain is universal.

Once developed, models can be used in three different ways. Models can be used for prediction, for description of the real world, or can be used to logically deduce the existence of phenomena that have not been observed in the real world. One of the main themes of the previous chapter was that different models will be desirable for different purposes, and each of these three purposes will call for different types of models. This idea lays a foundation for future chapters, when the types of models appropriate for various purposes will be discussed.

Models can be developed by logically deducing them from a theoretical beginning, or by observing empirical regularities in the real world. While models are developed both ways, ultimately every model must have its foundation in some empirical regularity. The real world is complex, and knowledge about it cannot be developed without some observations of real-world empirical regularities. From there, a theory might be developed and its logical implications tested, but the original theory must find its roots in empirical observation rather than logical deduction. Economics is an empirical science.

This idea deserves further discussion, and will be elaborated and examined in detail in the next chapter on deductive and inductive reasoning in economics.

NOTES

1. Some individuals in the hard sciences reject the use of models except as heuristic devices. See Mary B. Hesse, *Models and Analogies in Science* (Notre Dame, Indiana: University of Notre Dame Press, 1966) and W. H. Leatherdale, *The Role of Analogy, Model, and Metaphor in Science* (Amsterdam: North-Holland, 1974) for a discussion of the issues.

2. See Mark Blaug, *The Methodology of Economics* (Cambridge: Cambridge University Press, 1980), p. 4n.

3. These are paraphrased dictionary definitions.

4. Abraham Kaplan, *The Conduct of Inquiry* (San Francisco: Chandler, 1964), calls these general principles laws and distinguishes them from facts (which are not general) and models (which are analogs to the real world).

5. See Donald McClosky, *The Rhetoric of Economics* (Madison: University of Wisconsin Press, 1985) for an interesting and insightful discussion of the rhetoric of economics.

6. Ludwig von Mises, *Epistemological Problems of Economics* (New York: New York University Press, 1981), pp. 13–15, argues that theoretical understanding must precede empirical observation.

7. This is, of course, the thrust of the extensive literature seeking the micro-foundations of macroeconomics.

8. Theoretical relationships have been contrived in this case, but the point is that the empirical model could exist without a theory to explain it.

9. Note, however, that Karl R. Popper, *The Logic of Scientific Discovery* (New York: Basic Books, 1959), p. 73, states that axioms are not self-evident.

10. Another common axiomatic framework in economics takes downward-sloping demand curves to be axiomatic. Edward R. Morey, "Confuser Surplus," *American Economic Review* 74, no. 1 (March 1984), pp. 163–73, discusses some of the implications of this in comparison to assuming a utility function. This is discussed at length in Chapter 7.

11. This point was made long ago by W. Stanley Jevons, *The Principles of Science* (London: MacMillan and Company, 1887), p. 627.

12. It is worth noting that these three uses of models consider only the positive aspects of economics. From a normative standpoint, the conclusions of the models could be used to make policy prescriptions, to advise individuals on optimal courses of action, and so forth. Such normative uses require accurate models in a positive sense to be effective, however.

13. Hayek has discussed simple and complex phenomena in this vein.

Chapter 4

INDUCTION AND DEDUCTION
IN ECONOMICS

All knowledge proceeds originally from experience . . . but one accidental observation well used may lead us to make thousands of observations in an intentional and organised manner, and thus a science may be gradually worked out from the smallest opening.

W. Stanley Jevons (1887, pp. 399–400)

May we venture to hope . . . that Inductive Reasoning, which has long been the glory of Science, will [cease] to be the scandal of Philosophy?

C. D. Broad (1926, p. 67)

Chapter 3 has already introduced the reader to the general direction that will be taken in the present chapter. There, it was argued that ultimately, economic knowledge is based on empirical observation of the real world. Observing specific real-world events and from that generalizing to events yet to be observed is inductive reasoning. Yet, it was also argued that economic models are not acceptable to contemporary practitioners of economics unless the model is based upon a theory. The theory, coupled with assumptions about the real world, produces the model; thus, the conclusions of the model are logically deduced. Since a theory is necessary for an acceptable model, the model is based on deductive reasoning. Combining these two lines of thought, any economic model is both deductive and inductive. There is no paradox here, because any model in economics must have been developed by a combination of inductive and deductive reasoning.[1] The use to which the model will be put will determine the appropriate doses of induction and deduction. While these are issues that economists do not often concern themselves with, later chapters apply the conclusions of this chapter, and the issues are directly relevant to current issues in economics. This chapter begins with an introductory discussion on the concepts of induction and deduction, which will provide the framework for the application of these ideas to economic models later in the chapter.

DEDUCTION AND ECONOMIC MODELS

Economists will find themselves familiar with deductive reasoning because economic models are presented in a deductive manner. Using deductive reasoning, one or more propositions, called premises, are used to demonstrate that other propositions will necessarily be true when the premises are true.[2] Following the terminology of the last chapter, the premises will be the axioms and assumptions employed in the model. Given the axioms and assumptions, it is simply a matter of logic to deduce propositions that are necessarily implied by the premises of the model. It is standard procedure in economics to present models deductively, stating the axioms and assumptions, and then deducing the conclusions. Frequently, a premium is placed on being able to derive the conclusions of a model mathematically, which means that the premises of the model are stated in mathematical notation; then they are manipulated mathematically to arrive at the model's conclusion. Thus, for example, William Brock praises a book in a book review, noting that the book's conclusions are demonstrated both graphically and rigorously.[3] Here, rigorously refers to the use of calculus and algebra, and one is left to wonder why a geometric proof is not rigorous.

For those familiar with the literature in economics, there certainly can be no question about the premium that is placed upon being able to demonstrate one's economic theories through the use of sophisticated mathematical tools. Economists in the 1950s and 1960s, following the example set by Samuelson,[4] were pioneering this type of analysis, and the premium placed on mathematical models is due in no small part to the successes that they and others working in a similar manner enjoyed following publication of their earlier works. The use of mathematics in economics helps to demonstrate the logical consequences of economic theories, helps to discover logical implications that are not always obvious without the mathematical demonstrations, and helps to define more precisely exactly what was meant by certain terms and ideas in economics. Indeed, the advances made in economics due to the use of mathematics are so evident that the use of mathematical models in economics certainly needs no defense.

The point to be made here, though, is that economic models by convention are presented in a deductive manner, and if the demonstration of the model is done via equations, rather than in graphs or verbally, so much the better. This shows the inherent truth of the model. Up to a point, this method of finding the truth can be defended. It does, after all, test the reasoning in the model for logical flaws. What it does not do, though, is examine the origin of the model's premises, or find all of the logically true propositions that follow from the premises. It also does not imply that the model originally was conceived through deductive reasoning. The model builder could have sensed the conclusions of the model through a flash of inspiration, or through the observation of some empirical regularity, and only then asked what axioms and assumptions would be needed to generate the conclusion. Reverse engineering can—and often is—done in economics.

This is not meant as a criticism, as will be seen later in the chapter. Although the rhetoric of economics is deductive, it is certainly valid to search for knowledge by seeking the necessary assumptions required to produce a particular conclusion. When finally presented for the world to see, the model will appear in its deductive form, but an inductive search may be the most fruitful way of developing the model.

There are really two related issues here. The first is whether economic knowledge is developed deductively or inductively.[5] That question was introduced in the previous chapter, and will be discussed further later in this chapter. The second issue is of more direct interest to the deductive methods discussed above. Since economic models are presented deductively, regardless of their origins, how are the assumptions and axioms chosen, and how is it decided which logical implications of the model to develop?

This question has two sub-parts. The first is which premises will be used to develop the model. The second regards the conclusions of the model. When many axioms and assumptions are used as premises, there are many possible logical implications of the premises. Typically, a model builder does not present every possible logical implication of the model, which leaves open the question about which logical implications will be presented.[6]

The contemporary paradigm in economics which relies on models that are presented deductively has answers for these questions. First, there are some axioms of economics that are taken as not subject to dispute by the model builder. These axioms may vary among schools of thought, but generally will be accepted, at least by the model builder and others sympathetic to the model builder's school of thought, as indisputable. Examples might be utility maximization, wealth maximization, downward sloping demand curves, and rational expectations. These examples are strategically chosen, since there are future chapters devoted to each one. It is also worth noting that some practitioners of economics might object to the axioms selected by others, but the details will be discussed later.

Certain axioms are selected as given by the model builder, then, leaving the determination of assumptions and the selection of logical implications as the next task of the model builder. Undertaking these tasks, however, is what is considered a research agenda in economics, and is the role of economic theorizing. Since there are many possible assumptions that could be made, and one model builder will be hard pressed to try them all, economic research consists of showing the implications of different assumptions. Furthermore, since any complex set of axioms and assumptions can lead to many logical implications, it is the role of economic research to ferret out new logical implications from previously used axioms and assumptions. Thus, while there is a specific question about how any one set of assumptions or logical implications is arrived at, the general answer is that it is the role of economic research to explore the various possible combinations of axioms and assumptions, and their logical implications.

In any particular case, however, the individual researcher has the task of selecting assumptions (and even axioms), and using them to discover some logical implications. How this takes place—and should take place—will be examined after some discussion on inductive reasoning.

INDUCTION

Induction is the inverse operation from deduction. Deduction begins with certain general principles, and from those principles infers conditions about specific cases. The premises are given, and then the conclusion is inferred. As already noted, economic theories are always presented in a deductive manner. A general theory is presented, which is then applied to the specific case at hand. Induction works the opposite way. The conclusion or outcome is given, and from that the premises are inferred. When applied to economic models, inductive reasoning means observing real-world behavior and from that arriving at the general theory that explains what is observed. As Jevons noted, "The truths to be ascertained are more general than the data from which they are drawn. . . . Given events obeying certain unknown laws, we have to discover the laws obeyed. Instead of the comparatively easy task of finding what effects will follow from a given law, the effects are now given and the law is required."[7] The reader will probably be sympathetic to Jevons's suggestion that induction is a more difficult process than deduction, but when only the results of a law can be observed and the law itself is unknown, the inquisitive individual will have little choice but to rely on induction to discover the underlying law.

There are two types of induction: perfect and imperfect. With perfect induction, all of the effects of the law in question can be observed; with imperfect induction on the other hand, only some of the effects can ever be observed. It should be apparent that induction in economics is imperfect induction. Some consequences of economic laws can be observed, but all consequences can never be observed. The fact that induction in economics must be imperfect induction is what makes the science of economics useful. One could, perhaps, be more confident of a theory if all of its real-world outcomes could be examined, but economic theory is useful precisely because it offers knowledge about events that have not yet been observed.

It is worth emphasizing that most knowledge about the real world is acquired inductively. One is confident that the sun will rise tomorrow morning based upon inductive reasoning, but would be hard pressed to come up with a logical proof that the sun must rise tomorrow. Boland argues that such a proof would not be possible.[8] Farmers plant their crops knowing that they will grow, and knowing the factors (drought, insects, and so forth) that can hinder their growth. A center fielder for a baseball team knows where to stand to catch a fly ball. Yet none of this knowledge is the result of deductive reasoning. Based on evidence from the experience of the past, inductive reasoning gives the farmer, the baseball player, and every individual most of the knowledge that they have about the real world. Indeed, it is not possible to observe a general law; only specific instances of that law at work can be observed.

This being the case, any knowledge about economics must ultimately have an inductive foundation. Empirical regularities are observed in the real world, and from these specific cases, general theories are inductively developed which explain how the specific cases are caused by a more general law.

INDUCTIVE AND DEDUCTIVE MODEL DEVELOPMENT

With this background, it is possible to describe the development of economic models, and to understand the roles of inductive and deductive reasoning. All knowledge in economics must ultimately have its foundation in the observation of empirical regularities in the real world. These empirical regularities are the facts that the economist must explain. The economist then uses inductive reasoning to try to discover what premises would be consistent with the empirical regularities that have been observed. Once discovered, these premises form the axioms and assumptions of the economic model. The reasoning is inductive. This is the foundation of the argument made in the previous chapter that economics is an empirical science. All economic theories must have an empirical foundation.

Once an economic theory has been proposed, other economists will want to be assured that the conclusions of the model really do follow from its premises, so the economist presents the model to other economists in a deductive manner, stating that if the premises can be taken as given, the conclusions logically follow. This does not mean that the model was developed deductively; only that it can be presented that way. It was noted earlier that deduction is in general a much easier process than induction, so for the sake of clarity (and perhaps persuasiveness), it makes sense to present the logic of the model the easy way—deductively—even though it may have been discovered the hard way.

This argument certainly does not imply that all economists arrive at all of their discoveries inductively. There are many regularly accepted axioms and assumptions frequently used by economic theorists. It is a legitimate and often fruitful activity to take some combination of these axioms and assumptions to use as premises for a model, and then to use deductive reasoning to arrive at some implications. The argument here says only that those axioms and assumptions originally must have been discovered inductively.

To work deductively, some premises must be taken as given. To work inductively, some premises must be discovered that logically can produce the effects trying to be explained. In both cases, premises are needed, even though in the first case they are assumed and in the second case they are derived. However, all premises are not equally acceptable. In a new area of inquiry, the observation of empirical regularities will lead to hypotheses. As more evidence is gathered, hypotheses that are regularly supported by the data, and which enable predictions that are eventually shown to be true, are elevated to the status of theories. Successful theories may even reach the point where practitioners are willing to take their conclusions as axiomatic. Thus, for example, utility maximization, wealth maximization, downward sloping demand curves, and rational expectations have all been used as axioms in economic models.

To build a model deductively, the model builder must take as given the premises that are already well accepted by economists. This permits economists to better understand the logical implications of the premises generally accepted by the profession.

Indeed, unless generally accepted premises are chosen, the model could be called deductive, but probably could not be called economics. Economists over the centuries have built up a large body of knowledge, and economics consists of extending that knowledge, which means that the premises taken as given must conform to those premises that economists are willing to accept as given.

The same considerations hold for inductive models. From observed effects, the economist must discover their causes, but acceptable causes must be those that other economists would be willing to accept as axioms or assumptions. For example, it would not be acceptable to develop a logically consistent theory that sunspots cause business cycles,[9] even though it is plausible that solar activity might affect human behavior, which could in turn have an effect on the economy. While it is logically possible, there has not been sufficient empirical evidence, so sunspots cannot be used as a premise in a model. In short, there is no difference between acceptable premises in inductive or deductive models, and this is especially obvious since even models that are discovered inductively must be presented deductively to conform to the standards of the profession.

Economic models must have an inductive foundation, since the origin of the premises of a model must be inductive. Deductive reasoning provides a method of model validation in economics, though, and so is an indispensable part of economics. The general principles that have an inductive origin will be considered valid only if the effects that are observed in the real world can be deductively derived from premises generally believed to be valid by the profession in general. It is only through deductive proof that a model can be shown to be valid.

While logical proofs might be verbal, graphical, or mathematical, the decades since World War II have seen an increasing preference for mathematical proofs. This may in part affect what is accepted as evidence, but economics relies heavily on evidence that can be readily quantified. Theories might be developed about lesser-developed countries, or more urban areas or more liberal political views, but the theories will be more persuasive if the theorist is able to come up with cardinal values to quantify the theory's implications. Everybody may know what a developed country is, or an urban area is, or a political liberal is, but a theory will be more successful if its implications are more readily quantifiable.

There is good reason for this in that it enables the theory to be more easily extended to new real-world situations. A theory may predict a more extensive development of property rights under certain conditions, but the more readily measurable the development of property rights is, the more easily the theory can be applied to new situations.

Theories are developed by observing real-world events, but there are many ways to observe the real world. One way is to look out the window. Despite its lack of sophistication, much can be learned this way. Another way is to find readily quantifiable events to observe, and to systematically look for relationships that might exist. With the development of the computer, modern econometrics has made this method much easier to pursue. There is a separate chapter devoted to the role of econometrics in economic models, but the basic argument in that chapter is that econometrics is essentially a technique for looking at the world, just as looking out the window is. Perhaps it is more sophisticated, but fundamentally, it is a way for observing systematic relationships in the real world, and can be used to generate theories inductively. The comparative difficulty of inductive reasoning has already been noted, so the investigator should welcome the additional tools that modern econometrics has to offer.

Along these lines, a passage written by Jevons in 1887 is of interest. Jevons notes that given the laws of multiplication, multiplying is a deductive process, whereas finding factors is an inductive process that attempts to discover the numbers that, when multiplied, yield a particular result. Jevons[10] remarks,

Given any two numbers, we may by a simple and infallible process obtain their product; but when a large number is given it is quite another matter to determine its factors. Can the reader say what two numbers multiplied together will produce the number 8,616,460,799? I think it is unlikely that anyone but myself shall ever know; for they are two large prime numbers, and can only be rediscovered by trying in succession a long series of prime divisors until the right one be fallen upon. The work would probably occupy a good computer for many weeks, but it did not occupy me many minutes to multiply the two factors together.

The two numbers are 89,861 and 96,079. When Jevons in 1887 referred to a good computer, he was referring to an individual, and not the IBM PC that found the factors in under half an hour, including the time it took to write the program. The same program that found the factors also confirmed Jevons's assertion that the factors themselves are prime numbers.

It may be interesting that the computer can perform this inductive type of task that during Jevons's lifetime would not have been possible, but the example serves to illustrate in general the power of the computer to aid in inductive problem solving. Stuffed with data, the computer has the ability to find empirical relationships relatively painlessly, and newly discovered empirical regularities are the raw material that can be used for new theory and model development. Viewing econometrics as just another method of looking at the world, similar to peering out a window, it is apparent that the modern computer can be of great assistance in the development of economics through induction. Like any tool, it can also be misused, however. At this point, the relationship between econometrics and inductive model development can be observed. The separate chapter on the use of econometrics will discuss the relationship further.

LAW AND ECONOMICS: A DIGRESSION

Perhaps no discipline embodies the spirit of inductive reasoning more than law. In the development of the common law, the general law is developed based upon outcomes in specific cases. Presumably, all cases are determined by the same laws, but the laws are never explicitly stated in the common law. Instead, the precedent set by earlier cases is used as a foundation for deciding present cases according to the underlying general laws. While this discussion digresses from the topic of model building in economics, it is a good enough discussion about the application of inductive reasoning to be worth some space.[11]

The law can be developed in two ways. A legislature can pass statutes declaring certain rules to be laws, or courts can make decisions in specific cases which will then be used as precedent in future cases. The first type of law is statutory law; the second type is common law. In countries like the United States and Great Britain, most laws are developed through the common law rather than by statute.

The common law works in the following way. A case comes to court, at which time the court renders a decision in a specific case. The court's object in rendering a decision is to embody the general rules of the common law in the decision, even though common rule laws are not explicitly written down in any one place. At a later date, another case may come to court that has circumstances similar to the earlier case. The decision in the new case will be rendered according to the precedent set in the earlier case. As additional cases are decided, the court will render its decisions based on the precedent of the cases that have gone before. Presumably, the cases are decided according to a general rule, but the general rule is only implied in the cases that have gone before. Thus, legal reasoning is entirely inductive. The legal question is to find the outcome in this specific case that is consistent with the outcomes in previous cases, even though the general principle is not stated anywhere, and probably could not be.

The reason is that many legal questions, because they deal with nuances of the real world, can be very complex. Any explicitly stated general principle would out of necessity leave out some of these complexities—assume them away—simply because it is not possible to take account of every unforeseen circumstance. Because a law cannot state every condition that might be relevant, it is in effect a model, and the same limitations that apply to models, as discussed in Chapter 2, also apply to explicitly written laws. The common law deals with this by not writing out the law explicitly, but instead lets the implied principles in earlier decisions serve as a guide for making legal decisions in the future.

The English language uses the same word to describe legal laws and physical laws, and while the two types of laws have their differences, there is also a common ground. The courts, in the common law process, seek to discover and apply the true law, while the physical scientists also seek to discover and apply the true law. An important difference is that the law is applied to what F. A. Hayek has called complex phenomena,[12] and because of the complexity of the phenomena involved, the discipline must rely more heavily on inductive reasoning to try to find unifying principles for seemingly diverse special cases. Many writers have commented on the efficiency of the common law process,[13] and the reason why it works efficiently is that the subject matter is so complex that it would be impossible to state the general law that would take account of all of the complexities in the real world.

The implications of this discussion for economics echo the conclusions of Chapter 2. Because models are simplifications of reality, no model can be appropriate for every application. A legal statute, as a model of the legal principle, will have to assume away some real-world complexities, and so can never be appropriate for every case. Thus, with statutory laws, court interpretations are frequently necessary, for just this reason. Likewise, no economic model can completely capture all of the economic nuances of the real world. When anomalies arise, the task of the researcher is to put together a plausible model that explains the anomaly while preserving the generally accepted principles of the discipline.

Economics relies heavily on inductive reasoning for the development of general principles. So does law. Both deal with complex phenomena, but an important difference is that when anomalies appear in economics, the models can be easily modified to encompass a more general set of circumstances. It is more difficult to change the law, so its practitioners cannot afford the luxury of frequent legal change; thus, much law is left embodied as principles implied in a body of special cases, rather than explicitly stated.

FINDING THE TRUE THEORY

Following on the heels of the section on inductive reasoning in the law, one might wonder, if the actual law cannot be explicitly stated, how one could ever find the true law. Perhaps the answer is that the true law is too complex to ever be explicitly stated with all of its nuances intact; perhaps the answer is that there is no true law. The same question might be asked of economics. How does one find a true theory? Does deductive reasoning have any claim over inductive reasoning in identifying theories that are true?

Deductive reasoning has an inherent advantage over inductive reasoning in that it enables the theory to be tested to see if it is logically consistent; in other words, it reveals that the theory's conclusions actually are logical implications of the premises. As was argued earlier, this is why theories are presented in a deductive manner rather than in an inductive manner. Deductive reasoning does not necessarily expose all of the logical implications of a theory's premises, though, so while some implications of a theory may be shown deductively to follow from the premises, there may be other implications, as yet undiscovered, that are contradicted by real-world experience.

In this case, inductive reasoning shows its advantages by finding the premises that are necessary to imply the implications of a theory, since it is the implications rather than the premises that are taken as given in induction. But there may be many possible sets of premises that could generate particular observed real-world outcomes, so induction cannot infallibly produce a true theory either.

The brief answer to the question posed by this section is that logic cannot identify a true theory, if by true theory one means a theory that correctly identifies causal factors and their effects in the real world. Inductive reasoning can identify the premises that are consistent with observed phenomena, and deductive reasoning can identify implications that logically follow from a theory's premises, but none of this says anything about the real world. A theory can be logically true, but false as a description of real-world events. The reason is that there is an infinite number of sets of premises that are logically consistent with a given set of real-world outcomes, and it is not possible to use logic to identify the true set of premises.

Even this statement is not strong enough, though, for there never actually is a true set of premises—in the sense that the set of premises can be guaranteed to produce an accurate model of real-world events under all conditions. Models, after all, are simplifications, and must necessarily leave out some of the complexity of the real world. As such, when the complexity that is left out in one case becomes important in another, the theory behind the model no longer seems to work. In one way this might be viewed as a problem with the theory, but seen in another light, no theory can be expected to work in every instance, because the simplifying assumptions necessary to the theory must exclude some instances. Because of this, it really does not make sense to say that a logically consistent theory is true or untrue. Rather, the theory either applies well to a particular case, or it does not. In short, simply because of the nature of a theory, a theory can never in the strict sense be said to be true.

This being the case, the theorist is left with the task of selecting (or constructing) the best theory for the application at hand. Finding the correct theory really means finding the theory that works best for the intended application. Of course, one will hope that the theory is not only consistent with the past but will also explain similar future occurrences, and perhaps more importantly, will be able to identify ahead of time those situations where the theory will not apply. This requires domain assumptions that are clearly identified as such. A discussion of this topic leads directly to the next chapter on positivism.

CONCLUSION

In economics today, models are not acceptable without theories to back them up, and the convention in modern economics is to present the logical structure of the model deductively, presenting what almost amounts to a fiction of model building. Research findings are presented deductively even though the original knowledge was gained inductively. The reason for this is that the deductive presentation of a model allows an easy method for the model builder to demonstrate that the conclusions of the model logically follow from its premises.

Despite the fact that economic models are presented in a deductive manner, all economic knowledge ultimately has its roots in inductive reasoning. Economic theory attempts to organize and explain empirical regularities in the real world, so the ultimate source of economic knowledge must be the observation of the regularities, followed by the inductive reasoning that would enable a small group of premises to explain many diverse phenomena. It is not possible to use deductive reasoning to arrive at the premises of a model.

Because models are simplifications of the real world, no model can be expected to explain every possible real-world occurrence. This will be true even when all of the stated premises of the model appear to be valid, because there is always the unstated premise that nothing outside the model will intervene. Since models are simplifications, the real world must contain something outside the model, which leaves open the possibility that despite valid premises, the logical conclusion of the model will differ from the occurrences in the real world. Thus, while logic can show that a model's conclusions are consistent with its premises, logic can never demonstrate that a model is a true representation of the real world.[14] To the contrary, logic can demonstrate that a model that will always yield truthful predictions can never be produced. Since a model necessarily leaves out some elements of the real world, it is always logically possible that one of the unrepresented features of the real world will cause the model's predictions to be invalid. It is not enough to assume all other things held equal, because other things are always changing, and the complete theory would have to completely enumerate what things must remain unchanged, and what things could change without affecting the model's outcome. Such a complete enumeration would not be possible.

Ultimately, then, to brand a theory as true or false is an oversimplification. A theory may be more or less appropriate for a particular task, but a test of the logical consistency of the theory will not reveal its appropriateness. The obvious next step is to identify how the appropriate theory for a particular application can be identified. This leads directly to the next chapter on methodological positivism.

NOTES

1. Gordon Tullock, *The Organization of Inquiry* (Durham, N.C.: Duke University Press, 1966), makes a similar observation by suggesting that deductive reasoning is implied in any act of induction. "From this observation and a general principle that, if two things are correlated, they are probably causally related with the probability proportional to the strength of the correlation, we deduce a causal relation" (p. 113).

2. The ideas of deduction and induction presented here are not new, and follow the concepts as outlined by W. Stanley Jevons, *The Principles of Science* (London: Macmillan and Company, 1887).

3. William A. Brock, "Contestable Markets and the Theory of Industry Structure," *Journal of Political Economy* 91, no. 6 (December 1983), pp. 1055–66.

4. Paul A. Samuelson, *Foundations of Economic Analysis* (Cambridge, Mass.: Harvard University Press, 1947).

5. This question is, of course, just a subset of the question of how knowledge is in general developed. Jerrold J. Katz, *The Problem of Induction and Its Solution* (Chicago: University of Chicago Press, 1962), reviews the issues in detail.

6. See Martin Ricketts, "Tax Theory and Tax Policy," in Alan Peacock and Francesco Forte, eds., *The Political Economy of Taxation* (New York: St. Martin's Press, 1981), pp. 29–46, for some implications of the optimal tax literature that are often ignored.

7. W. Stanley Jevons, *The Principles of Science*, p. 122.

8. Lawrence A. Boland, *The Foundations of Economic Method* (London: George Allen and Unwin, 1982), p. 14.

9. See David Cass and Karl Shell, "Do Sunspots Matter?" *Journal of Political Economy* 91, no. 2 (April 1983), pp. 193–227.

10. *The Principles of Science*, pp. 122–23.

11. See Holcombe, *Public Finance and the Political Process* (Carbondale: Southern Illinois University Press, 1983), chapter 9, for some background discussion on the subject.

12. *Studies in Philosophy, Politics, and Economics* (Chicago: University of Chicago Press, 1967), chapter 2.

13. Regarding the efficiency of the common law, see Holcombe, *Public Finance and the Political Process*, chapter 9; Richard A. Posner, *Economic Analysis of Law* (Boston: Little, Brown, 1972); Paul H. Rubin, "Why Is the Common Law Efficient?" *Journal of Legal Studies* 6, no. 1 (January 1977), pp. 51–63; and George L. Priest, "The Common Law Process and the Selection of Legal Rules," *Journal of Legal Studies* 6, no. 1 (January 1977), pp. 65–82.

14. This statement must exclude tautological models, which do have a role in economics. See the chapter on utility and entrepreneurship below.

Chapter 5

POSITIVISM

> Viewed as a body of substantive hypotheses, theory is to be judged by its predictive power for the class of phenomena which it is intended to "explain."
>
> Milton Friedman (1953, p. 8).

Perhaps no single work on the methodology of economics has been more influential than Milton Friedman's essay, "The Methodology of Positive Economics."[1] The roots of methodological positivism lie outside economics,[2] but since Friedman's essay, the debate on the applicability of positivism to economics has been continual and lively, and shows no signs of slowing down.[3] The present chapter will evaluate the doctrine of methodological positivism using as a foundation the material discussed in the previous chapters. Methodological positivism provides a guideline for model selection, which is the problem frequently deferred earlier in the book. Much was said about using the appropriate model for the circumstances, but little was said about how the appropriate model was to be found. This chapter, along with Chapters 6 and 7, deals directly with the issue of selecting the appropriate model for the circumstances. The criterion for model selection according to the positivist doctrine is the model's ability to predict. The most appropriate model is the one that gives the most accurate predictions.

Friedman's essay, and indeed the whole positivist doctrine, is subject to debate on how it should be interpreted. Rather than enter into this type of debate, the present chapter will examine the doctrine using as a foundation the discussion of models from Chapters 2, 3, and 4. If the material from those chapters can be accepted, then some implications regarding the positivist doctrine logically follow.

FINDING THE APPROPRIATE MODEL

Models, it has been extensively argued, are simplifications of the real world, and as a result, no single model can ever hope to depict accurately all real-world phenomena. The nature of a model precludes this. Thus, the model most appropriate for describing one phenomenon will not be the most appropriate for describing all phenomena, and nobody should expect it to be. This led to the conclusion in Chapter 4 that there is no such thing as a true model, only a model that is appropriate for the circumstances at hand. A model might be thought of as true in the sense that for a particular circumstance, it accurately depicts the relationship between two variables,[4] but this can be misleading, because the relationship may change under different circumstances, and it in no way tests the veracity of the assumptions made in the model. A researcher might like to think that he or she has discovered the true model, but it is more accurate to consider the model appropriate for the particular instance, rather than true.

This leads to another issue discussed in Chapter 4. The real world is a complex place, and a model attempts to make a simplified depiction of it. For any particular observed real-world effect, there will always be many possible logically consistent causal factors. Due to its simplifying assumptions, a model eliminates some of these possible causal factors, even though they cannot be rejected on logical grounds alone. Thus, the researcher must have some reason to believe that the causal factors depicted in the accepted model are in fact the most important ones. To discuss this in the terms used by Jevons a century ago,[5] if perfect induction were possible, then it would be possible, at least conceptually, to develop a model that would accurately depict all of the phenomena under question. Since the real world is complex, and since economic models are intended to apply to situations that have not yet arisen, perfect induction will never be possible. Some logical explanations will have been assumed away, and some events that the model is intended to explain have yet to happen. Thus, models developed inductively will rely on imperfect induction, and deductively developed models will admit the possibility that some causal factors assumed away in the model are more significant than those being modeled.

Chapter 4 noted that in the real world, most people arrive at most of their knowledge about the world through imperfect deduction. They observe phenomena, and then formulate explanations that are consistent with the phenomena. These explanations contain assumptions about the world, of course, and the assumptions can be used to formulate additional conclusions about the world. Further, the model of the world can be examined deductively to make sure that it is logically consistent, but the model is originally developed through imperfect induction, and the ultimate foundation must remain on these grounds, since it will never be possible to observe all possible cases, especially in the social sciences.[6]

Jevons uses this idea as an introduction to the concept of probability. He argues: "All our inferences concerning the future are merely probable, and a due appreciation of the degree of probability depends upon a comprehension of the principles of the subject. I am convinced that it is impossible to expound the methods of induction in a sound manner, without resting them upon the theory of probability. Perfect knowledge alone can give certainty, and in nature perfect knowledge would be infinite knowledge, which is clearly beyond our capacities. We have, therefore, to content ourselves with partial knowledge—knowledge mingled with ignorance, producing doubt."[7] This emphasizes the idea that one cannot conclude that beyond a doubt the true model of anything has been found, and foreshadows the idea in twentieth-century economics that the applicability of a model can and should be an empirical question. Rather than concluding that a model is true, one must conclude that it is probably accurate in this instance.

If the conclusions of a model turn out to be robust—that is, true in many instances—one might be inclined to generalize the model's conclusions to events not yet observed. Since the model predicted accurately before, it will probably be accurate in the future. This view of economic models treats future events like the balls in an urn in a statistics problem. If the researcher has reached into the urn five times before and drawn a red ball, then the next ball drawn will probably be red also. If economic events can be treated in the same way, then the test of an economic model is its ability to predict. The ball and urn analogy, of course, is simply a model of the doctrine of methodological positivism, and as such contains simplifying assumptions. The distinction between simple and complex phenomena is an important one, and will be examined next.

SIMPLE AND COMPLEX PHENOMENA

Frequently, analogies are drawn between models in physics and models in economics. Milton Friedman uses several such examples in his essay. Indeed, there is a significant parallel, but there is also an important difference which deserves recognition. In physics, the underlying structure of the phenomena to be analyzed does not change, while in economics, such changes are more common, and are even to be expected. This is what Hayek is referring to when he discusses the differences between simple and complex phenomena.[8] Because of this, methodological positivism may be more appropriate to sciences like physics than to economics. In some sense, the best model in physics is the one that gives the most accurate predictions, especially when prediction is the goal of the model. However, in economics, the best model may not be the one that predicts the best, even when the goal of the model is prediction.[9]

An example from physics may serve as an illustration. Newtonian physics is able to describe mathematically physical relationships, such as the relative motions of objects. Within the realm of the phenomena being observed before 1900, Newtonian physics predicted well. However, more precise measurements revealed slight contradictions in the Newtonian system that laid the groundwork for Einstein's theory of relativity.[10] The Newtonian models that predicted well under some circumstances (and are still used to model those circumstances) did not do well under other circumstances. The result, of course, was the development of new models to explain the new circumstances.

Some reflection on the reason for the development of the new theory is in order here. The old model predicted fine under the old circumstances, and is still useful in those circumstances, but the results of the old model did not extrapolate to some circumstances beyond its range of observation. When the goal is prediction, interpolation of data seems to work well, but extrapolation is prone to failure. This is, of course, not a new insight.

In physics and in economics, theories are developed assuming that all other things are held equal. In the physical sciences, however, there are relatively few causal variables, and all can be easily defined, so that the assumptions of all other things equal can be readily verified. In other words, it is relatively easy to identify when conditions in a physical science have changed, thus alerting the researcher to the possibility of different results under the different conditions. In the social sciences (and biological sciences as well), phenomena are more complex. There are more interrelated variables, and frequently some variable omitted from the model may well have an effect on the model's outcome. This is true in the physical sciences as well, to a degree, but in the physical sciences it is easier to identify a change in the factors outside the model.

The result of this is that in economics it is more important to have a theory behind the model. In a positivist sense, one of the most successful models in physics is that of gravity. It predicts very accurately, over a wide range of circumstances from minute particles to galaxies. Yet there is no theory behind it. Gravity is understood only as a mathematical relationship between objects. While constant mathematical relationships seem to exist in the physical world, they do not appear in the social world. Social phenomena are more complex. For example, the Phillips curve was treated by some economists as a constant relationship after its discovery, but a decade after the constant relationship was discovered it was gone. If conditions had remained the same as they were before 1960, the Phillips curve would not have disappeard, but things are always changing, and it is important to understand what conditions must remain the same.

Consider the following example. A man drops an iron ball from a railroad bridge onto a concrete highway below. He performs the experiment several times, always observing the same result. He then concludes that iron balls tend to move from railroad tracks to concrete roads. He then finds a concrete bridge over the railroad, and expects the iron ball to be pulled from the tracks to the bridge above. Two things can be observed from this example. First, as long as all roads travel under railroads, the man's theory will predict perfectly. In the physical world where it is relatively easy to see when the conditions of an experiment change, a simple model describing the relationship will work fine without a theory explaining why the relationship holds. The experimenter can say, "This relationship seems to hold when roads pass under railroad bridges; now I want to see if the relationship still holds when the railroad is under the road." When he discovers the opposite relationship, he has the data to show that in fact the iron ball always falls down. This model is adequate for most purposes, but when he discovers that the motion of planets can be described by a similar model, he will now realize that the iron ball and the Earth are attracted to each other, so that the Earth actually approaches the ball too, although by an immeasurably small amount.

This much observed about the physical world, the second thing to observe is that the example does not extrapolate very well to a social science example like the Phillips curve. The original model above was that of a ball being attracted to a concrete road. It is relatively easy to see the difference in the experiment when the ball is dropped to the road and when the ball is expected to go up to the road from underneath. Now consider the Phillips curve relationship. What conditions must change in order for that relationship to be altered? It is impossible to tell without a theory to explain the relationship, since things are always changing in the social world, and it is not clear what the causal factors are without a theory. With complex phenomena, as in the social sciences, it is necessary to have a theory in order to be confident of the validity of a model, even if the model has predicted well in the past.

TESTING ASSUMPTIONS

In Friedman's famous essay, he has much to say about the fact that the validity of assumptions cannot be ascertained—indeed has no meaning—outside of the context of the model in which the assumptions are used. The model's assumptions are tested by the ability of the model to predict. Alan Musgrave[11] has added considerable clarity to Friedman's claim by carefully delineating types of assumptions. Musgrave's taxonomy of negligibility assumptions, domain assumptions, and heuristic assumptions has been used in earlier chapters.

Within this taxonomy, the perils in accepting literally the positivist conclusion that the test of a model is its ability to predict lies in the realm of domain assumptions. Negligibility assumptions recognize the possibility that a certain factor might exist, but assert that the effect of the factor will be negligible on the outcome of the model. Thus, a model predicting the effect of an increase in the price of steel on the quantity of bicycles demanded might ignore a retail sales tax, even though sales tax is charged on bicycles. The argument would be that sales tax can be safely left out of the model because it will have a negligible impact on the model's results. Heuristic assumptions in a model employ premises that are not true, but that do not affect the outcome of the model.[12] For example, the bicycle market may be assumed to be perfectly competitive even though firms have some obvious latitude in the prices they charge. If the assumption does not affect the outcome of the model, then its use is appropriate.

How is one to tell if the assumptions are appropriate? Herein lies the positivist test. If the model predicts well, then the assumptions are appropriate. Friedman has done an excellent job of defending this position, so only a brief sketch of his argument should be necessary. With examples from the physical sciences, Friedman notes that such assumptions can only have meaning within the context of a model, and that the assumptions that may be appropriate for some models will not be appropriate to others.

Friedman's example of the effect of the resistance of air on falling bodies is a good one. Bodies accelerate at 32 feet per second per second when dropped to Earth in a vacuum. An iron ball dropped from a second story window will fall to Earth as if it is in a vacuum. Thus, to estimate the ball's speed at any time during its fall, the assumption that the ball is in a vacuum is used. The effect of air resistance is negligible, so air resistance is assumed to have no effect as a negligibility assumption. The same experiment done with a feather would yield a different result. Thus, the same assumption cannot be employed in this case.

A model necessarily employs simplifying assumptions. How can one know whether an assumption is appropriate or not? Again, the positivist test is the ability of the model to predict. Can the effects of air resistance be assumed away? If the model predicts well with the assumption, then the positivist answers yes.

The positivist answer is appropriate for negligibility and heuristic assumptions, but not necessarily for domain assumptions. Consider the above experiment again, this time performed in a vacuum. Both the feather and the iron ball hit the ground at the same time according to the model that neglects the effects of air resistance. The assumption of no air resistance is a negligibility assumption for the iron ball—it does not matter whether the ball is dropped in a vacuum or not—but it is a domain assumption for the feather. If the feather is dropped in the domain of a vacuum, then it will accelerate at 32 feet per second per second, but if air resistance is present, it will fall more slowly than predicted.

Clearly, if a domain assumption is violated, then the model is inappropriate. A positivist might argue that only by empirical observation can one tell that the domain assumption is violated. For example, there is never a perfect vacuum, and a positivist might argue that the assumption of a vacuum simply amounts to the empirical question of how close to a vacuum one must be before a body will fall as if it is in a vacuum. Thus, there is a blurring between negligibility assumptions and domain assumptions. The presence of some air will have a negligible effect on the feather, but more air will constitute a domain outside of which the model is not valid.

Despite this argument, however, there is a clear conceptual difference between negligibility and domain assumptions. A negligibility assumption means that it does not matter whether the model considers the factor or not, whereas a domain assumption means that the model holds only as long as the factor in question is outside the domain of the test. This is an important difference.

Therefore, assumptions in a model do matter, and in particular, domain assumptions must be carefully understood. A model that applies under one set of circumstances may not apply under another. It was illustrated above that there is not a clear line between negligibility assumptions and domain assumptions. This can be especially perilous, because a factor may not be included in a model under the assumption that its effect will be negligible. The model may fit the data well, and yet if the assumption is in fact a domain assumption, a change in the factor in question may cause a model that predicted well in the past to predict poorly in the future.

Another peril is that for both negligibility and domain assumptions, most of the assumptions in the model will not be explicitly stated. A model is necessarily a simplification, and the real world is too complex to make an extensive list of all of the factors that are assumed not to affect the model. Thus, some important domain assumptions may go unrecognized in any model.

Can a model be tested by its ability to predict? Only in a limited sense. Heuristic assumptions in a model are the easiest to deal with, because they are always explicit. Negligibility assumptions are the things left out of the model because they have no appreciable effect. With both of these types of assumptions, the ability of a model to predict is a test of the appropriateness of the assumptions. With domain assumptions, however, this is not the case. If a domain assumption is made explicitly, then it may be easy to tell when it is violated, and take the appropriate action, either modifying the model, or replacing it. However, when domain assumptions are implicit and unrecognized, as some always must be, or when they are confused with negligibility assumptions, a model that has a history of accurate prediction may not predict well in the future.[13]

The conclusion must be that a model cannot be judged solely on its ability to predict, if by ability to predict one means its historical record of prediction. In addition to the demonstrated predictive content of a model, the applicability of the model's domain assumptions must also be considered. Thus, the assumptions of a model do matter, and frequently the most important assumptions in a model will be the unstated (and perhaps unrecognized) ones.

In economics, models are sometimes developed with the goal of prediction, and it is possible to extrapolate past trends. Methodological positivism would suggest that the best model is the model with the best record of prediction, but there may be good reason for selecting a model that does not predict as well but that has more realistic underlying assumptions. The reason is that prediction in economics is extrapolation, and the circumstances that existed at the time the data were accumulated may change in future periods. There are not economic constants in the same sense that there are physical constants.[14]

A good example of the problems that can arise in applying methodological positivism in economics is the use of the Phillips curve, as noted earlier. Phillips found and reported a stable inverse relationship between changes in nominal wages and unemployment,[15] and shortly thereafter, other papers replicated his study, using other countries and other data representing inflation or a close relative of inflation. An empirical regularity was discovered relating unemployment and inflation, and the empirical relationship was convincing enough[16] that economists were willing to accept the Phillips curve model, because it predicted well. Samuelson and Solow even referred to a Phillips curve as "the menu of choice between different degrees of unemployment and price stability."[17] The model predicted well for the period prior to 1970, but fared poorly after that.

With some hindsight and further analysis, it is now apparent that the theoretical framework behind the Phillips curve was unrealistically simple considering the data being analyzed. Just as Newtonian physics predicts well under certain conditions, so does the Phillips curve model. However, in physics it tends to be easier to tell when conditions have changed, compared to economics. Economic models, when used for prediction, are always extrapolating, so it is always important to consider the appropriateness of the underlying assumptions in addition to the past predictive ability of the model. At the simplest level, an appropriate economic model cannot be chosen based solely on its past predictive ability. The Phillips curve episode makes this clear by example, and the reason behind the Phillips curve episode is the complexity of the ceteris paribus conditions that permeate economic models.[18] There is, indeed, good reason for examining the realism of assumptions in economic models, and in particular, the appropriateness of the domain assumptions to the problem at hand.

In this discussion, the predictive ability of a model has been equated with its past record of predictions. With regard to the Phillips curve, its record was good before 1970, but has been poor since. As a result, the simple positivist criterion of predictive ability, if used in 1970, would have led to the acceptance of a model that would have fared poorly after 1970. Needless to say, the evidence since 1970 would have to lead the positivist to reject the simple Phillips relationship as a good model of the relationship between inflation and unemployment.

When a positivist considers the predictive ability of a model, does this mean the past record of predictive accuracy, or the model's expected future predictive ability? The answer must be the past record, for the future ability of the model to predict cannot be known ahead of time. Of course it is a model with the ability to predict accurately in the future that is the goal of the modeling process, but the only criteria available now are the model's present characteristics. For the positivist, the key criterion is predictive ability, which must mean how well the model has predicted in the past, since no future predictions are available in the present.

The main argument here is that domain assumptions are critical to the future success of a model, so the model must be assessed on the basis of its domain assumptions in addition to other criteria. A positivist would reject this idea, arguing that the validity of a model's assumptions can only be tested by the ability of the model to predict. If a model predicts well, then its assumptions are valid. But while this is a good test for negligibility and heuristic assumptions, the predictability test does not test domain assumptions.

Another important but distinct aspect of positivism is the idea that theories can never be proven to be true; they can only be demonstrated to be false. This deserves mention, for completeness, in a chapter on positivism, but at this point will only be noted in passing. Chapter 10, on empirical work in economics, discusses the subject more completely.

CONCLUSION

The chapters leading up to the present one have argued that models represent simplifications of the real world. The real world is too complex to be understood in its entirety. Models, by representing only a small portion of the real world, make the relationships being modeled more easily understood. Because models leave out aspects of the real world, no single model can accurately represent all real-world phenomena. As a result, a model that is well suited for one purpose will be inappropriate for other purposes, so one important task of the researcher is to pick the model appropriate for the purpose at hand.

One criterion that has been suggested for selecting the appropriate model is the predictive ability of the model. This doctrine of methodological positivism argues that the validity of a model's assumptions cannot be judged independently of the predictive content of the model in which they are used. Models, by their very nature, are unrealistic, and it is their very unrealism that makes them valuable in understanding real-world relationships. The more accurately a model's conclusions mimic the real world, the more accurately the model is able to isolate the most important causal elements. The assumptions of a model cannot be judged independently of the model's predictive ability.

The criterion of predictive ability is appropriate as a guide for the inclusion of negligibility and heuristic assumptions in a model. If a factor is present but assumed away, or if an unrealistic condition is assumed to exist and the model predicts accurately anyway, then these factors do not affect the model's ability to accurately depict the real-world relationships among variables. The same cannot be said with regard to domain assumptions, because domain assumptions assert that the conclusions of the model hold as long as the factor assumed constant in fact does not change. A model that predicts well in one domain may not predict well in another.

The problems with domain assumptions can be minimized if the most important ones are explicitly stated. This way, it will be obvious when the domain assumption is violated and the model is no longer applicable. However, the real world is very complex, and it would be impossible for a model to list all of its domain assumptions. As a result, a factor included in a domain assumption may change without the user of the model being aware of it, and a model that once predicted well may no longer yield accurate predictions. Another possible problem is that a domain assumption may be confused with a negligibility assumption. A researcher may believe that a factor may be safely left out of a model because its effect would be negligible, when in fact a change in the disregarded factor may produce a real world outside the domain in which the model has predictive ability.

The ultimate conclusion is that assumptions do matter, and that assumptions must be evaluated outside of simply examining their predictive ability in a model. It is not easy to evaluate the assumptions of a model, however, because in the vitally important area of domain assumptions, most assumptions necessarily will have to remain unstated due to the fact that the real world is too complex for the model builder to list (or be aware of) all of the factors that are assumed constant in the model. In addition, the model builder may be unable to distinguish domain assumptions from negligibility assumptions. Clearly, some criteria outside the predictive ability of a model must be used to evaluate the appropriateness of the model. The next two chapters address this issue.

This chapter has focused on the role of assumptions in models, but positivism is also closely related to the empirical testing of models. Empirical models are discussed in Chapter 10, and the discussion there is closely related to the positivism covered in this chapter. Before getting into the empirical issues, however, there is more to be said about assumptions in economic models.

NOTES

1. The essay is found in Friedman's *Essays in Positive Economics* (Chicago: University of Chicago Press, 1953), pp. 3–43.

2. See, for example, Karl R. Popper, *The Logic of Scientific Discovery* (New York: Basic Books, 1959), for a discussion of the issues as they relate to the philosophy of science.

3. Three recent books, Mark Blaug, *The Methodology of Economics* (Cambridge: Cambridge University Press, 1980), Lawrence A. Boland, *The Foundations of Economic Method* (London: George Allen and Unwin, 1982), and Bruce J. Caldwell, *Beyond Positivism: Economic Methodology in the Twentieth Century* (London: George Allen and Unwin, 1982), discuss many of the issues and provide numerous references to support the assertion of a lively debate.

4. The concept of a true model is used in econometric modeling, and will be discussed in the chapter on empirical work. This seems to be the notion of truth used by econometricians.

5. W. S. Jevons, *The Principles of Science* (London: MacMillan and Company, 1887).

6. See F. A. Hayek, *Studies in Philosophy, Politics, and Economics* (Chicago: University of Chicago Press, 1967), chapter 2, who notes the differences between the social sciences and the natural sciences on this point.

7. William Stanley Jevons, *The Principles of Science* (London: MacMillan and Co., 1887), p. 197.

8. See Hayek, *Studies in Philosophy, Politics, and Economics* (Chicago: University of Chicago Press, 1967), chapter 2.

9. See Mario Rizzo, "Praxeology and Econometrics: A Critique of Positivist Economics," in Louis M. Spadaro, ed., *New Directions in Austrian Economics* (Kansas City: Sheed Andrews and McMeel, Inc., 1978), for an argument criticizing positivism on strictly logical grounds.

10. See Max Born, *Einstein's Theory of Relativity* (New York: Dover, 1962), for a complete discussion.

11. Musgrave, " 'Unreal Assumptions' in Economic Theory: The F-Twist Untwisted," *Kyklos* 34, Fasc. 3 (1981), pp. 377–87.

12. As noted previously, the concept of a heuristic assumption differs slightly here from Musgrave's use, and Musgrave would be likely to call the example used here a variant of a negligibility assumption. The difference in uses does not affect these general conclusions, however.

13. As applied to macroeconomic policy making, see Robert E. Lucas, Jr., "Econometric Policy Evaluation: A Critique," pp. 104–30 in his *Studies in Business Cycle Theory* (Cambridge, Mass.: MIT Press, 1981).

14. For a related discussion, see Thomas F. Cooley and Stephen F. LeRoy, "Identification and Estimation of Money Demand," *American Economic Review* 71, no. 5 (December 1981), pp. 825–44.

15. A. W. Phillips, "The Relation Between Unemployment and the Rate of Change of Money Wage Rates in the United Kingdom, 1862–1957," *Economica* 25 (November 1958), pp. 283–99.

16. However, there was also a theoretical underpinning for the data. See Robert Lipsey, "The Relationship Between Unemployment and the Rate of Change of Money Wage Rates in the United Kingdom, 1862–1957: A Further Analysis," *Economica* 27 (February 1960), pp. 1–31.

17. Paul A. Samuelson and Robert M. Solow, "Analytical Aspects of Anti-inflation Policy," *American Economic Review* 50, no. 2 (May 1960), pp. 177–94.

18. See Cooley and LeRoy, "Identification and Estimation of Money Demand," *American Economic Review* 71, no. 5 (December 1981), pp. 825–44, on this point.

Chapter 6

METHODOLOGICAL INDIVIDUALISM

> In studying the actions of individuals, we also learn everything
> about the collectives and society.
>
> Ludwig von Mises (1962, p. 81).

This chapter deals with the characteristic of methodological individualism in a model as a criterion for evaluating the appropriateness of the model. Methodological individualism refers to the use of the individual as the fundamental unit of analysis in a social science. Many of the arguments employed in previous chapters have applied to scientific inquiry in general. The arguments in this chapter apply only to the social sciences; in Chapter 7, the applicability is further narrowed to economics alone. The argument that methodological individualism is a criterion for model evaluation is not meant to imply that it is the only criterion that should be used. However, it will be argued that a foundation of methodological individualism is significant enough that one should be suspicious of any economic model that cannot trace its foundations back to the behavior of individuals. The argument will be built upon the foundation laid in earlier chapters.

Models are necessarily simplified views of the real world. Certain factors are assumed away in order to make the model tractable. The previous chapter argued that domain assumptions pose special problems to the economic model builder. A model's conclusions will be applicable only under certain conditions. These conditions constitute the domain of the model, and domain assumptions specify the conditions. Several problems with domain assumptions were noted in the previous chapter, but the most significant is that because the real world is so complex, and because so many things are always changing, it will be impossible for the model builder to list explicitly all of the domain assumptions built into the model. The model specifies certain premises and arrives at certain conclusions, and those real-world factors not covered in the model are assumed to have no effect. If a factor in the real world changes that is left out of the model as a domain assumption, then the model that applied to the previous domain will no longer be applicable.

A major hazard exists because it is not possible to list all of the model's domain assumptions, or even be aware of them, due to the complex nature of the real world. This means that the model builder always runs the risk that a model that works well today may be inappropriate in the future due to a change in a factor covered by a domain assumption. Further, since most domain assumptions, of necessity, will be implied rather than explicitly stated, the model builder may not even be aware of the change until after the model ceases to accurately depict real-world events. Ideally there should be some way to provide assurance to the user of a model that it will not become obsolete and inappropriate without warning.

There can be no absolute guarantees, but some assurance of the generality of a model can be provided in two ways. The most obvious is that any important domain assumptions recognized by the model builder be stated explicitly. This, as already noted, is not always easy. The second is to build upon a framework that has an easily understandable and readily acceptable foundation, and that makes any domain assumptions placed on top of the foundation readily obvious. This is the role of methodological individualism. When a model is built upon the behavior of individuals, it is relatively easy to see if that behavior is approximately consistent with the observed real-world behavior of individuals. Furthermore, domain assumptions built upon this foundation will be more apparent. Thus, it will be easier to judge the reasonableness of the assumptions, and it will be easier to detect when a domain assumption is violated.

The defense of methodological individualism as an important foundation for an economic model finds its origins in the development of the current economic paradigm. Assumptions that have attained the status of axioms are not easy to find, but they must be at the foundation of any model that claims to yield predictions about the course of future events.

THE ECONOMIC PARADIGM

Ludwig von Mises, in his introduction to *Human Action*, offers some insightful comments on the origins of economics and on the significance of economics when compared to other bodies of knowledge. Mises argues that economics is the youngest science because the discovery of laws that regulated social interaction went beyond the limits of previous knowledge to open up a new field of study. Whereas previously, social philosophers had dealt with holistic concepts such as nations, races, and even humanity as a whole, economics discovered laws that regulated human interaction. Social institutions were constrained to be consistent with these laws, and could not arbitrarily be designed by social reformers. Before economics, social problems were viewed as ethical problems that could be overcome with better citizens. The discovery of economic laws that governed the interaction of individuals changed this view of society.[1]

Mises makes several important points. First, Mises makes the distinction between economics and all other areas of inquiry by noting that economists have developed general laws of social interaction. These regularities in social phenomena are the foundation of what is thought of as economics: they constitute the paradigm of economics. Thus, economics is more than just the study of economic phenomena. For example, history and accounting are two disciplines distinct from economics that also study economic phenomena, although from a different perspective and using different methods. Likewise, economic imperialists have branched into studying diverse phenomena such as law, family interactions, and even biological phenomena, but using the economic method founded upon the discovery of general laws of social interaction.

Mises also suggests that methodological individualism is at the foundation of the economic method of inquiry by noting that previously philosophers had treated social groups as a whole rather than considering the group's behavior to be the result of the behavior of individuals within the group. Economists do consider the behavior of groups, certainly, such as suppliers, demanders, and markets. But the group behavior seen in markets can be traced back to the behavior of the individuals who trade in those markets, and Mises saw the great contribution of economics as being able to understand that the behavior of individuals has implications for the behavior of the group. Group behavior is simply the aggregated behavior of individuals; the group as a unit exhibits no behavior beyond the individuals that compose it.

These observations are not intended to be taken as proof of anything, but rather are intended as a starting point for considering the role of methodological individualism in economics. It seems undeniable that the goal of modern economics is the discovering and understanding of regularities in social phenomena. It seems less obvious that methodological individualism is at the foundation of that understanding, particularly since the macroeconomics of the 20th century has started from a distinctly nonindividualistic foundation. Microeconomics, in contrast, is almost synonymous with economic theory that is aggregated from the foundation of individual behavior.

If the actual paradigm of economics is being considered, then, methodological individualism does not appear to be a requirement. But when the origins of the economic paradigm are considered, methodological individualism plays an indispensable role. Adam Smith's greatest insight was that individuals pursuing their own self-interest produce a social order that was no part of their intentions.

The marginalist revolution late in the 1800s was also built on a foundation of methodological individualism, and neoclassical economics clearly followed in the same tradition. The only significant deviation from the tenets of methodological individualism since the birth of economics has been the Keynesian macroeconomics born in the 1930s. This macroeconomics has yielded valuable insights, beyond a doubt, so would seem to argue against methodological individualism as a foundation of the economic paradigm. Thus, some discussion devoted specifically to the Keynesian revolution is warranted. But first, by way of summary, it is instructive to note that in general, significant developments in economics have been built on a foundation of methodological individualism, and indeed, if it were not for the remnants of Keynesian economics, methodological individualism could be declared a part of the current economic paradigm. Perhaps the Keynesian revolution is called a revolution rather than being viewed as evolution precisely because it departs from the methodological individualism present in the paradigm that existed when the revolution began.

KEYNESIAN ECONOMICS

If its name has any validity, the Keynesian revolution must date back to 1936 and the publication of Keynes's *General Theory*. The followers of Keynes proceeded to develop a macroeconomic theory distinct from the economics that had preceded it, and the old theory, still developing, took on the moniker of neoclassical economics. Following Keynes, the neoclassical economics was viewed to be a special case of the more general macroeconomics, but this was not proven to be so. This will be discussed further below.

The Keynesian theory remained separate from neoclassical economics throughout the 1950s, and in the late 1950s incorporated a breakthrough connecting it more to the real world: the Phillips curve, named after its discoverer.[2] The empirical finding of a stable and inverse relationship between inflation and unemployment was generalized into an integral part of the Keynesian theory, and was the foundation of Keynesian economic policy that was used most prominently in the 1960s. Perhaps the best illustration of this is the labeling of a Phillips curve by Paul Samuelson and Robert Solow as a "menu of choices" between inflation rates and unemployment rates.[3]

From a methodological standpoint, the Phillips curve episode is interesting for at least two reasons. First, it is an example of an empirical regularity that found theoretical foundations without being based on an individualistic theory. Second, it is an example of a theoretical relationship that was originally discovered through empirical observation.[4]

Although Keynesian economics was used as a policy tool throughout the 1960s, macroeconomics and microeconomics remained completely separate, despite the notion begun by Keynes that the neoclassical framework was but a special case of his general theory. Early in the 1970s some economists were sufficiently curious about this that they began looking into the microfoundations of macroeconomics.[5] They reasoned that if macroeconomics and microeconomics were both accurate descriptions of the economy, they ought to be logically consistent with each other. Explicit connection of the theories would confirm that consistency, and places where the theories were inconsistent could help to develop both macroeconomics and microeconomics.

This line of inquiry brought about significant changes in macroeconomic theory over the next decade and a half. One branch of this line of inquiry was the development of the monetarist school of macroeconomics as a viable alternative to Keynesianism. Monetarism predates the explicit search for microfoundations,[6] but modern monetarism is noteworthy because of its consistency with neoclassical microeconomics. It is interesting to consider the interaction of monetarism with the discovery of the Phillips curve, because it lends some insight into the way in which methodological individualism has affected the development of macroeconomics. This will be considered below.

First, another branch of the microfoundations of macroeconomics deserves mention. The rational expectations school, finding its foundations in a paper by Muth,[7] discards entirely theories based on misperceptions by economic actors and disequilibrium phenomena to place macroeconomics squarely on the same foundations as microeconomics.[8] The search for microfoundations for macroeconomic theories, including monetarism and rational expectations, has produced major changes in macroeconomic theory through the 1970s and 1980s. It is interesting to observe that while there have been advances in microeconomics over that time, the changes have been evolutionary and the neoclassical foundations have remained. This stands in contrast to the major changes that have occurred in macroeconomics. This section has given a brief account of the facts. The next section considers the methodological implications.

METHODOLOGICAL IMPLICATIONS

Keynesian economics is not built upon a foundation of methodological individualism, and the Phillips curve that was a cornerstone of Keynesian economic policy was not even generated from the Keynesian theory. Rather, it was an empirical observation later shown to be consistent with the Keynesian model. After the fact, economists have argued that acceptance of Keynesian economics as a national policy has been counterproductive on several grounds. First, it could not work once people understood the policy.[9] Second, the policy recommendations themselves provided intellectual foundations for politically irresponsible behavior.[10] Other charges might be made against Keynesianism, and all of the charges might have refutations, but the point in this chapter on methodological individualism is not to debate the merits of Keynesianism, but rather to see if more careful adherence to individualism might have avoided some of the problems brought about by Keynesianism. Note, however, that while traditional Keynesian economics is without an individualistic foundation, Keynes himself, in the *General Theory*, was very concerned with the individual behavior underlying aggregate phenomena. The lack of methodological individualism must be attributed more to Keynes's followers, then, than to Keynes himself.

The first methodological point to consider when relating the Keynesian revolution to the lack of individualistic foundations in the models is that Keynes and his followers brought insight to macroeconomic phenomena that had not previously existed. On this point alone one would not want to have seen the Keynesian theory rejected on methodological grounds, because of the implication that the accompanying insights would have been lost as well. This point is not irrefutably true, since it is possible that the insights would have been generated with other models that were not considered due to the influence of Keynes. However, there is a valid argument that when searching for knowledge, one never knows where it might arise, so this is a reason for leaving open all avenues of inquiry and avoiding methodological imperatives.

The second methodological point is that the Phillips curve was originally an empirical observation, then linked to the Keynesian framework, and again without individualistic foundations. One might argue that economic policy based on the Phillips curve was counterproductive, using this as an example of applying theories without individualistic foundations. The monetarist theory of the vertical long-run Phillips curve, with Phillips's original curve just being a short-run trade-off, eventually replaced the Keynesian variant, and this would seem to show the virtue of building a theory on individualistic foundations, as the monetarists did, rather than on the behavior of aggregates, as in the Keynesian theory.

The monetarist theory arose as a response to the Keynesian Phillips curve, however, so the argument could be made that the monetarist theory never would have emerged were it not for the Keynesian theory that apparently needed refutation. It takes a theory to beat a theory, and it may be that if the Keynesian Phillips curve had not risen to prominence, the monetarist version never would have been invented. Again, it appears to be throwing away knowledge to reject a theory on methodological grounds. This should not, however, discourage someone from attempting to place a more solid methodological foundation under a theory. This was precisely the goal of those individuals who were (and are) seeking microfoundations for macroeconomics.

After the fact, however, it appears to the critics of Keynesianism that the entire theory was built upon faulty premises. The experiences with Keynesian economic policy in the 1960s and 1970s, for example, seem to soundly refute the Keynesian policy prescriptions developed earlier. Many observers in the 1980s would argue that the world would have been better off without Keynesian economic policy in the 1960s and 1970s. Without debating this point, would the world have been better off without the Keynesian theory, independent of its policy? Should the theory have been rejected on methodological grounds because it was not based on methodological individualism?

In fact, the theory was modified, if not rejected, on just those grounds, as was noted above. The monetarist and rational expectations theories saw problems with Keynesianism and placed the microfoundations under the theory, changing it in the process. With hindsight, one might have wished for these developments to have come sooner, but the changes that have occurred in macroeconomic theory have been methodological at their foundation, and have been based on the principle of methodological individualism. In retrospect, beneficial insights resulted from the development of Keynesian economics, despite its lack of individualistic foundations. Also in retrospect, economists should have been more suspicious of the general applicability of the theory since it was not shown to be consistent with the rational behavior of individuals. This theme will be reconsidered after looking in more detail at the concept of methodological pluralism.

PLURALISM

Methodological pluralism ". . . takes as a starting assumption that no universally applicable, logically compelling method of theory appraisal exists."[11] The title of Caldwell's book, *Beyond Positivism: Economic Methodology in the Twentieth Century*, from which this definition of pluralism is taken, is worthy of note because Caldwell, who advocates pluralism, echoes the sentiments of methodological writers in the 1980s, and the title is very descriptive.[12] Friedman's influential advocacy of positivism established it as the stated methodology of economists up through the 1980s, and indeed economists who have not specifically studied methodological issues tend to view positivism as the methodological foundation of economics.[13] Among methodologists, however, positivism has lost favor and pluralism has replaced it.

Some support for pluralism can be found in the digression on Keynesianism just undertaken. Indeed, much was learned within the aggregated Keynesian framework, from the search for empirical regularities that established the notion of the Phillips curve, and from the search for individualistic foundations for macrotheory. Given the fruitfulness of various approaches, one could hardly argue for restricting the search for knowledge on methodological grounds.

Caldwell's examples suggest that the pluralism he refers to aligns closely with schools of thought, like neoclassical, Keynesian, Austrian, and rational expectations. The conclusions would generalize, however, to methods of inquiry such as mathematical, empirical, and so forth, as well. There seems to be no good reason to exclude any avenue of inquiry.

Mark Blaug extends this notion to methodological individualism explicitly. He argues that while methodological individualism is to be commended as a heuristic device, it is clearly not necessary as a foundation for economic knowledge,[14] and points out the useful theories that have been developed without it as evidence of his argument. The arguments are persuasive, and must be taken even more seriously since the doctrine of pluralism has replaced positivism as the methodology of choice.

Pluralism itself is not actually a methodology, of course, but a call to abandon methodological prescriptions. The pluralists argue that there is not a true best methodology, and that even if there were, we could not identify it if we saw it. Therefore, any defense of methodological individualism must be carefully made in light of the arguments of methodologists, and especially in light of the advances in economics that have been made outside the individualistic framework. The next section turns to this task.

IN DEFENSE OF METHODOLOGICAL INDIVIDUALISM

The arguments of the methodological pluralists are well taken, and it is necessary to point out that this section does not disagree with them. Indeed, knowledge should be accepted by whatever method it can be found. But while theories not based on individualistic foundations cannot be rejected out of hand, individualistic theories are resting on much firmer ground, and as a result should be more readily accepted into the mainstream of economic knowledge. The basis of this argument is found in the material from earlier chapters.

The following ideas have been established earlier. First, economic models are of necessity a simplification of reality. All models are. Therefore, no model can accurately depict every possible phenomenon. The right model is a function of the circumstance in which it is to be used, so, because models are simplifications of reality, no model will yield true predictions under every conceivable circumstance. The assumptions of the model must first be met.

Second, it was argued that all of the assumptions of a model can never be enumerated. Negligibility and domain assumptions leave out many factors and restrict the model to certain circumstances, but because of the complexity of the real world, all of the circumstances under which the model does not apply cannot be listed. This leaves open the possibility that the model may surprise the model user on occasion by not accurately depicting the real world when it was expected to. Ideally, a model should keep such surprises to a minimum.

Third, it was argued that domain assumptions are especially troublesome in this regard. In the natural sciences, the domain under which a model is expected to be accurate will be more easy to ascertain, because there are far fewer domain variables to be concerned with. In the social sciences, the environment is complex and is subject to the sometimes difficult task of modeling the behavior of individuals, making the domain of a model less clear. As a result, assumptions can be important in determining the generality of a model's predictions. The less sure the model user is of a model's domain, the less sure the user can be of the predictions of the model.

Domain assumptions are important, then, but how is one to identify some domain assumptions as better than others? A good way to do so is to, whenever possible, use assumptions that have proven to have had general applicability in the past. The economic framework of individuals pursuing their own self-interest has held up well for over two centuries, and in a wide variety of applications. As a result, when the utility maximizing framework is applied to a new problem, the knowledge that economists have accumulated for centuries can be applied to the new application, thus lending confidence to the generality of the new model's conclusions.

The argument in favor of methodological individualism, then, is not that it must be used to derive economic knowledge, but rather the more modest one that one can have more confidence in the generality of a model's conclusions when it rests on an individualistic framework. This argument does not imply that there is anything inherently superior about models that are built on an individualistic framework (although there may be), but rather that individualistic assumptions have stood a test of time and have shown themselves to be robust. Therefore, one can have more confidence in the results yielded from using a well-known tool with well-established properties rather than a tool with relatively unknown properties.

The development of Keynesian economics—and the concept of the Phillips curve in particular—can illustrate this point. While one cannot deny the useful findings of Keynesian economics, one can also see that the model was misleading to policy makers and economic forecasters alike. In particular, there clearly is not a stable trade-off between inflation and unemployment as was thought during the 1960s, and perhaps more important (though also more controversial), the fiscal policy implied by Keynesian theory will not have the effects it is predicted to have once individuals in the economy understand how the government is behaving. Advances in both of these areas were made by abandoning the aggregate approach of Keynesianism and building models on a foundation of rational individual behavior. The aggregate Keynesian models provided insight, to be sure, but the search for microfoundations for the models provided additional insight and overturned some of the notions thought true based solely on the aggregate approach.

The Phillips curve illustrates the same idea with respect to the identification of empirical regularities. Phillips discovered a regularity that dated back over a century, yet a decade after its discovery it was gone. The reason for its disappearance was understood once the empirical regularity was modeled using a framework of methodological individualism, but was not understood within the aggregate Keynesian framework. So while useful knowledge can be found in models outside the individualistic framework, an economist should be skeptical of such models until they are demonstrated to be consistent with rational individual behavior. Note that the Keynesian framework was detached from individualistic foundations for decades, but has benefitted greatly from the search for its individualistic roots.

The argument favoring methodological individualism, then, is not an argument that this is the only acceptable way to pursue economic knowledge, but it is an argument in favor of being skeptical of models not founded on individualistic postulates, and it is also an argument in favor of searching for individualistic foundations for models that do not yet have them. Without these individualistic foundations, an economist must be skeptical of a model's conclusions.

CONCLUSION

Methodological individualism is the cornerstone of economic analysis. Ever since Adam Smith's observation that each individual, pursuing his own self-interest, is led by an invisible hand to further goals that were not part of his intentions, economics has based the bulk of its theories on models depicting rational individual behavior. There have been exceptions, but even the most prominent exception—the development of Keynesian macroeconomics—provides lessons that support methodological individualism. Individualism is not a methodological imperative, but in social science a model not based on individualistic foundations must generate more skepticism about its conclusions, and there is, therefore, good reason for seeking individualistic foundations for theories that do not already have them.

Methodological pluralism advocates no constraints on the methodology employed by economists. If by this the pluralists mean that knowledge can be generated within a variety of methodological frameworks, then there is no conflict with methodological individualism. If the pluralists mean that one cannot tell ahead of time what fruitful avenues of inquiry will be, and that none should be shut off on methodological grounds, then there is no conflict with methodological individualism. But none of these pluralistic conclusions imply that one methodological foundation is as good as any other, and on this ground, methodological individualism has much to recommend it as the true methodological foundation of economics.

The argument regarding the virtues of methodological individualism is that individualism has proven itself to be a robust framework for economic analysis. While it may not be intrinsically superior to other methodological foundations, it has stood the test of time in proving its worth as a foundation for economic knowledge. When the results of a model can be traced back to the rational behavior of economic actors, then the economist can have more confidence in the model because this methodological foundation has proven so successful in the past in such a wide variety of applications. Without individualistic foundations, one cannot be sure how general the applicability of a model's conclusions are.

The problems of nonindividualistic models go back to the domain assumptions within the models. With models based on economic aggregates or on empirical regularities, there is no guarantee of the generality of the models' results. One can have more confidence with individualistic models because of the robustness that models based on like foundations have shown over the centuries. Keynesian macro models illustrate the case, by contrast, of models not based on an individualistic foundation that can be accepted for decades without individualistic ties, yet the incorporation of methodological individualism into the macro models has had a profound influence on the shape of macroeconomics.[15] While methodological individualism is not a methodological imperative, it is a superior methodological foundation simply because economists know so much about it.

This conclusion follows directly from the material of earlier chapters. Models are necessarily unrealistic and one model cannot be suited for every task because of the necessary simplicity of a model when compared to the real world. Therefore, assumptions do matter in the sense that the assumptions of a model must be chosen to be consistent with the task to be modeled. While one can never be completely sure that a model will accurately model the real world, models based on individualistic foundations stand a better chance of applying under changing domains, and of revealing themselves to be inappropriate ahead of time in those situations where the model will not be accurate. Economic models are built upon a foundation of assumptions. For any but the most trivial modeling exercise the scope of assumptions made about the real world will be too broad to enumerate. A model that uses unorthodox assumptions or is constructed in an unorthodox framework may predict well, yet it will have a significant drawback because its assumptions have not shown the robustness of models that have been demonstrated to be applicable in a wide variety of settings.

There is a methodological prescription that arises out of this chapter. Use models founded on methodological individualism when possible, and search for individualistic foundations for models that do not already have them.

NOTES

1. Ludwig von Mises, *Human Action*, Third Revised Edition (Chicago: Henry Regnery Company, 1966), pp. 1–2.

2. A.W. Phillips, "The Relation Between Unemployment and the Rate of Change of Money Wage Rates in the United Kingdom: 1862–1957," *Economica* 25 (November 1958), pp. 283–99.

3. Paul A. Samuelson and Robert M. Solow, "Analytical Aspects of Anti-inflation Policy," *American Economic Review* 50, no. 2 (May 1960), pp. 177–94. See also Robert Lipsey, "The Relationship Between Unemployment and the Rate of Change of Money Wage Rates in the United Kingdom, 1862–1957: A Further Analysis," *Economica* 27 (February 1960), pp. 1–31, for a development of these same ideas.

4. For a good history of the development of the Phillips curve theory, see Nancy J. Wulwick, "The Phillips Curve: Which? Whose? To Do What? How?" *Southern Economic Journal* 53, no. 4 (April 1987), pp. 834–57.

5. The key work beginning this literature is Edmund S. Phelps, et al., *Microeconomic Foundations of Employment and Inflation Theory* (New York: W.W. Norton, 1970).

6. An important contribution to this literature is Milton Friedman, "The Role of Monetary Policy," *American Economic Review* 58, no. 1 (March 1968), pp. 1–17.

7. John F. Muth, "Rational Expectations and the Theory of Price Movements," *Econometrica* 29, no. 6 (July 1961), pp. 315–35.

8. A key paper in this literature is Robert E. Lucas, Jr., "An Equilibrium Model of the Business Cycle," *Journal of Political Economy* 83, no. 6 (December 1975), pp. 1133–44.

9. See Robert E. Lucas, Jr., "Econometric Policy Evaluation: A Critique," in Karl Brunner and Alan H. Meltzer, eds., *The Phillips Curve and Labor Markets* (Amsterdam: North Holland, 1976), pp. 19–46, for this argument.

10. See James M. Buchanan and Richard E. Wagner, *Democracy in Deficit: The Political Legacy of Lord Keynes* (New York: Academic Press, 1977).

11. Bruce J. Caldwell, *Beyond Positivism: Economic Methodology in the Twentieth Century* (London: George Allen and Unwin, 1982), p. 245.

12. An influential book in this area is Paul Freyerabend, *Against Method* (Atlantic Highlands: Humanities Press, 1975), who argues that the only methodological principle that does not inhibit scientific progress is, "anything goes."

13. It is interesting to note, for example, that in a prominent introductory textbook, James D. Gwartney and Richard Stroup, *Economics: Private and Public Choice*, 3d ed. (New York: Academic Press, 1982), pp. 10–11, argue that positivism is a part of the economic way of thinking.

14. Mark Blaug, *The Methodology of Economics* (Cambridge: Cambridge University Press, 1980), pp. 49–52.

15. Again, note that while Keynesian models did not have individualistic foundations, Keynes himself, in the *General Theory*, was very concerned about the individual behavior underlying economic aggregates.

Chapter 7

PRINCIPLES OF ECONOMICS

> In the economist's own language, he must allocate the limited re-
> sources available to him for a particular study in the most efficient
> manner, which means considering just enough variables to obtain
> sufficiently accurate answers.
>
> Gary Becker (1971, p. 5).

In Chapter 6, methodological individualism was recommended
as a foundation for all economic models. This chapter looks into
the fundamental principles of economics in more detail. As was
suggested in Chapter 6, most economic models do use methodological individualism as a foundation. Nevertheless, they still
show a great deal of diversity, ranging from elegant mathematical
formulations to verbal descriptions of economic behavior. Some
models claim to discover knowledge through deductive reasoning based on principles known a priori to be true, while others
claim that answers to certain significant questions are ultimately empirical questions. Despite these methodological differences,
most economic models share a certain commonality in structure,
and this chapter will continue with an examination of some common elements in economic methodology.

Neoclassical microeconomics marks a common departure point
for most economic models. As noted in Chapter 6, an important
body of recent macroeconomics starts from this foundation, most
of microeconomics starts from this foundation, and even economists who choose to work outside the neoclassical framework
often find it useful to explicitly illustrate the differences, perhaps with critiques of the neoclassical paradigm as they depart
from it.[1]

The neoclassical framework begins with the concept of utility maximization or a derivative concept, that of the downward sloping demand curve. These two concepts—utility maximization and downward sloping demand curves—are virtually axiomatic in modern economics. An economic model builder may simply assume either one without justification, since they have long been established as well-known economic truths.

Much of this chapter is devoted to an analysis of these two concepts and the differences between them. The chapter also takes a look at comparative statics as a method of economic model building because the technique of comparative statics is as much a part of the economist's tool box as the downward sloping demand curve. Unlike the previous chapter, this one has nothing to advocate. It is simply an examination of some of the characteristics of the tools that economists use with enough regularity that they are often taken for granted.

DEMAND CURVES AND UTILITY FUNCTIONS

Following the textbook explanation of individual behavior in the neoclassical model, individuals have utility functions that exhibit certain properties. They are made up of indifference curves that cover every point in the commodity space and they order all points in the space. The ordering is transitive. Indifference curves exhibit diminishing marginal rates of substitution. Beginning with the utility function, neoclassical micro theory then derives the individual demand curve. The utility function or the demand curve derived from the utility function is used as the fundamental building block of a neoclassical model.[2]

Normally, analysis based on indifference curves and analysis based on demand curves will yield identical results, but this is not always the case. There is the celebrated (in theory) but ignored (in practice) Giffen's paradox, where a utility function generates an upward sloping demand curve, for example. Giffen's paradox arises because of a perverse interaction between the income and substitution effects in the utility function. The substitution effect always works in one direction for a change in relative prices. A decline in the relative price of a good makes it relatively cheaper, so the individual substitutes out of other goods and into the cheaper good, so a lower price increases the quantity that the individual demands. The converse is true for price increases.

For normal goods (in the technical sense used by economists), the income effect works in the same way. A decline in the price of a good gives the individual more purchasing power, and as a result of this increase in real income, the individual buys more of the good. But if the good is inferior (again, in the technical sense used by economists), the individual will buy less of it as the individual's income rises. As a standard example, if a person's income rises, the person will buy less hamburger and more steak. Therefore, if the price of hamburger falls, the person will buy more hamburger because hamburger is now relatively cheaper than other goods, but the person will buy less hamburger because the lower price of hamburger gives the individual more purchasing power. Whether the individual ends up buying more or less hamburger in total depends upon whether the additional hamburger purchased because of the lower relative price is sufficient to offset the reduction in hamburger purchased because of the increased income.

Most economists will assert that despite the possibility that the income and substitution effects may work in opposite directions, the substitution effect will always overwhelm the income effect so that for any good, whether normal or inferior, a lower price will increase the quantity that purchasers wish to buy. The bizarre instance where this is not the case is Giffen's paradox. Because of the ever present possibility of Giffen's paradox, some economists will claim that, for example, an increase in the price of a good could cause the quantity demanded for the good to either rise or fall. Because of the possibility of Giffen's paradox, the matter is an empirical question. Most economists, however, would reject an empirical finding of an upward sloping demand curve out of hand, and would claim that the demand curve could not have been estimated correctly. For this group of economists, the inverse relationship between the price of a good and the quantity demanded is axiomatic.

This would make it appear that if one were interested only in predicting the direction of change of some variable in response to a change in relative prices, one would only need to pay attention to the substitution effect. This statement as it stands is true, but if one wants the prediction to be correct, the income effect can sometimes overwhelm the substitution effect, so one cannot simply model economic behavior as if income effects do not exist.

This is most apparent in the analysis of labor supply. Assume, for example, that an income tax is increased. This lowers the return to work, so the individual will substitute out of work and take more leisure. However, the income effect could overwhelm the substitution effect and the individual could work more to try to make up for the lower after-tax income left due to the tax increase.[3] It is a standard demonstration to show that after the income tax, the individual could work more, less, or the same amount when compared to the before-tax situation.[4] Which result is correct is an empirical question.

The demand curve approach and the utility function approach are really two different ways of looking at economic phenomena, despite the fact that neoclassical microeconomists derive their demand curves from utility functions. In the demand curve approach, people always substitute into the cheaper alternative so any change in relative prices yields a straightforward prediction. In the utility function approach, the income effect may offset the substitution effect, so any question is an empirical question.

Earlier in the book it was argued that since any model is a simplification of reality, no model will be the perfect model for all circumstances, and that observation may be especially appropriate here. Sometimes income effects may be so insignificant that it is eminently reasonable to assume that people will substitute into the cheaper alternative, whereas at other times, income effects could be significant enough that the proper model must take them into account. Therefore, neither approach is being advocated, but the differences between the approaches bears some scrutiny. The role of economic theory in deriving policy implications revolves around these differences in an important way.

Consider for example the effects of a welfare program that pays larger benefits the lower an individual's income. This gives the welfare recipient the incentive to earn a lower income (since the program in essence pays the individual more the lower the individual's income). Therefore, the individual will work less.

This reasoning is based on the demand curve approach, though, where results always follow the substitution effect, but when income effects are taken into account, the individual might work more, less, or the same amount. This is really an empirical question.

THEORETICAL ISSUES AND EMPIRICAL QUESTIONS

The argument in this section has already been exposed in the previous section. Economic theory has great predictive ability. Indeed, based on only a few initial facts, economists are often willing to make sweeping predictions about the future consequences of those initial conditions. Tell an economist that a drought in Colombia has damaged this year's coffee crop and economists will be ready to predict that the price of coffee will rise, and since tea is now relatively cheaper compared to coffee, people will drink less coffee and more tea. Tell an economist that a blight has damaged the potato crop in Ireland and economists will be ready to predict that the price of potatoes will rise, and since beef is now relatively cheaper compared to potatoes, the Irish will demand less potatoes and more beef. Unless, of course, income effects are taken into account.

It is possible that potatoes make up a major portion of the Irish household budget at the time of the blight, and that the higher price causes such a reduction in income that the Irish demand more rather than less of the potato, if it is an inferior good in the technical sense of the word. In other words, anything can happen when income effects are included as a part of the analysis.

When neoclassical models are used as predictive devices, they do so based on the substitution effects, which unambiguously cause people to substitute into the cheaper alternative. Within this framework, marginal rates of substitution are the only things that matter. When neoclassical models cannot predict the direction of change, they are based on the utility function framework rather than the demand curve framework. No model that includes income effects can make an unambiguous prediction. In the worst case, one must always admit the possibility that a demand curve could slope upward, but income effects can be more benign than this and still allow ambiguity to cloud the predictions of a model.

Since income effects exist in the real world, how could one ever make a prediction based solely on a theory? If income effects are one of the many things that can be assumed away, then a theory with unambiguous predictions becomes a possibility.

These ideas fit nicely into the framework of Imre Lakatos, who argued that—contrary to Kuhn—theories can never be refuted because they are surrounded by a protective belt of assumptions.[5] One might imagine, for example, that a theory predicts something which turns out not to occur. The theory was not wrong; it simply did not account properly for income effects. This is powerful protection since the introduction of income effects always opens the possibility for any result.

Income effects are not alone here, and the chapter about theories of utility and entrepreneurship explores other assumptions that affect the ability of economic models to predict. However, the point of this section is to note that despite the neoclassical tradition of deriving the concepts of supply and demand from a foundation of utility maximizing behavior, the supply and demand framework has much more predictive content than the utility function framework which leaves everything as an empirical question.

The whole notion of predictive content of economic models is interesting enough to warrant further discussion regarding just what it is that economic models predict. The following discussion leaves behind the predictability of theories, for even if all questions are empirical questions in economics, empirical models predict too. But what do they predict?

PREDICTING BEHAVIOR AND PREDICTING CHANGES IN BEHAVIOR

Prediction is one of the many uses of economic models. Even after a model has been developed, it can be continually refined in order to yield ever more accurate predictions, or at least the forecaster would hope so. The quantity theory of money, for example, predates all living economists, yet is still undergoing refinement by current monetarists. Economists forecast a wide variety of phenomena, from interest rates, income, and inflation, to the demand for electricity and soft drinks.[6]

Consider for the moment an empirical model that estimates the demand for electricity. Presuming that it is a single equation model, the left side of the equation is the quantity demanded of electricity and the right side can be divided into two components: the independent variables and the error term. By refining the model to make it ever more accurate as a predictor, the error term will continue to decrease in magnitude, with the ultimate goal being to reduce it to zero. Considering the process in this setting, the error term appears to be only a collection of factors that have been left out of the model.

The reason why such a procedure can work to forecast electricity demand is that people do act according to quantifiable behavioral laws, and the purpose of the model is to depict these laws so that they can be extrapolated to future conditions. If the econometric ideal of reducing the error term to zero is in theory possible, then one implication of the foundations of this type of modeling is that individuals have no choice in their own behavior.

If, for example, an economist can predict how much electricity a family will use, then how can one meaningfully say that the family has any choice in the matter if the economist already knows what the family will do? One answer is that the economist cannot predict with certainty, but the modeler might respond that this is only because some elements of the true model are missing, and that if the model were completely specified, it would predict with complete accuracy. If such prediction would be possible, even in theory, then it appears that the individual has no choice.

This line of reasoning neglects the data that the model builder takes as given in order to build the model. In order to forecast the family's electricity consumption in the next period, the model builder used observations of the family's past behavior (along with observations on the behavior of other families) and was making the assumption that, given enough information, the family would act similarly in the future to the way that it acted in the past. But actions in the past were accepted as data rather than derived.

The point here is that prediction in economics is not prediction about what people will do, but rather is prediction about how peoples' behavior will change if certain conditions change. There is an important difference. The predictions are made based on the assumption that people will act in the future according to the same "laws" that they did in the past. The laws in fact do not compel people to behave that way, and often they do not. But if people are in general successful in acting to satisfy their ends with the means at hand, then it is reasonable to think that under similar future circumstances they will behave similarly.

At this point one could debate whether people actually have free will, or whether their future actions are already determined by the cause and effect nature of the universe. Such a debate is beyond the scope of this chapter (although a related issue will be undertaken in the next chapter). But how one answers this question should indicate whether one believes that the perfect empirical model with a zero error term is ever possible in theory. A step down from this lofty argument is the main point of this section. Economic models do not actually predict peoples' behavior. Rather, they start with past behavior and then predict how that behavior would change under different conditions.

DIFFERENCES IN TASTES

A related point was made by George Stigler and Gary Becker.[7] They consider the role of economic modeling once the process has reached a point where observed differences are the result of differing tastes among individuals. One way to handle such a situation is to accept that individuals are different and that once the problem has arrived at the point of differences in tastes, further analysis is not possible. This is similar to the observation made in the previous section that economic models forecast how individual behavior will change under new circumstances, given what it was in the past, rather than forecasting what individuals will do, purely and simply.

Stigler and Becker argue that the role of economics does not end once the model ceases to explain because of differences in tastes among individuals. Rather, economics is useful to try to explain those differences in tastes. Saying that individuals are different because they have different utility functions really amounts to saying that one does not know why individuals are different. In fact, different current preferences can often be traced back to different incomes or relative prices, either now or in the past.

One might observe, for example, that a person has a good deal of musical aptitude. This might result from innate ability, or perhaps from that person's enjoyment of music which caused the person to invest in learning it. These explanations amount to saying that we do not know why the person has a good deal of musical aptitude. But following Stigler and Becker, economic analysis does not have to end here. For example, one can observe that good musicians tend to come from families with musically active parents. This provides a musical background at an early age which lowers the cost of obtaining human capital in music, and with that background, causes the person to appreciate music more. Thus, what at first appears to be (1) innate ability or (2) personal preference could be (1a) a lower cost of obtaining human capital in the area and (2a) a background that enables the person to have the knowledge to appreciate music more. That is, what at first appears to be personal differences on closer inspection can be explained by a different set of relative prices facing the individuals.

Economic models that rest on a foundation of differentiating people by assigning them different utility functions, then, ultimately rely on noneconomic explanations of the phenomena under question. People are different, admittedly, but for economic models to depict them as having different utility functions avoids explaining the differences using economic principles. Limits to one's understanding might require that the problem be modeled this way sometimes, but assumptions that individuals are different should be recognized for what they are rather than taken as a final explanation. For example, a model might require the assumption that some people are risk averse while others are risk takers. Assumptions like this should prompt the model builder to ask what differences in incomes or relative prices could cause two otherwise identical individuals to act differently.

Individuals are different in the real world, but to assume that they have different utility functions in an economic model is to leave at least some of the causal factors outside the realm of economic analysis. Perhaps there are limits to what economic analysis can explain, but this should not discourage the curious economist from applying the tools of economic analysis to real-world phenomena rather than leaving the phenomena explained by factors outside the model.[8]

COMPARATIVE STATICS

Comparative statics is the fundamental method of economic analysis in the 20th century. While Chapter 6 debated the merits of methodological individualism, there is almost nothing to debate with regard to comparative statics. The most insightful economic models as well as those with the greatest predictive ability are built on the foundation of comparative statics. This is not a defense of comparative statics per se, except insofar as it is a method that has proven its merit over time when modeling a wide range of phenomena. Proponents and detractors of comparative statics all agree that it leaves out many aspects of economic behavior by showing the end points in a process without actually depicting the process that leads from one point to another. But the method can be defended in the same manner as other simplifying assumptions. The real world is complex and in order to model phenomena in an understandable way, some things must be omitted from the model.

Comparative statics really does not look at changes over time, but rather examines two different possible situations that hypothetically could exist at the same time. There is a certain price and quantity exchanged in the domestic coffee market, for example. If a tariff were placed on imported tea, this would raise the price of tea which would cause people to substitute into coffee. The increased demand for coffee would cause an increase in the price and an increase in the quantity exchanged. This illustration of comparative statics does not say that placing a tariff on tea will raise the price of coffee. It says that, if there were a tariff on tea, the price of coffee would be higher than it actually is at this moment. In other words, all other things held equal, an import barrier on tea will increase the price of coffee.[9]

One could easily imagine circumstances where a tariff is placed on tea and the price of coffee remains the same or even falls. Other things would have changed. This ceteris paribus assumption might be viewed as part of the protective belt of supply and demand analysis, but the characteristic that is of interest for the moment is the timelessness of the analysis. Comparative statics really compares two different hypothetical states of the world at the same time, or perhaps more accurately, without time.

Economics is not without dynamic models. Consider for examples the Austrian theories of competition and entrepreneurship[10] that look at the competitive process and growth theory that had its heyday in economics in the 1950s.[11] While these models provide insight into the way an economy works, they do not have the same predictive content as the comparative statics mainstays of supply and demand, utility theory, and the Keynesian macroeconomics that established itself so convincingly in the 1950s and 1960s. Economists have tried to incorporate time explicitly into economic models, but except for the principle of exponential growth upon which growth theory is founded, they have not had much success. And models based on the principle of exponential growth over time tend not to model economic change very convincingly. As might be expected, in these models the economy tends to be pretty much the same over time, except that it gets bigger.

This is not meant to criticize dynamic models, but it is meant to recognize their limited success in describing economic phenomena when compared to comparative statics models. Comparative statics is the method of contemporary economics, and comparative statics is a method that is devoid of time.

COMPARATIVE STATICS AND PREDICTION

The goal of prediction in economic models has been discussed in several different contexts previously. Within the positivist methodological framework, the ability to predict is the ultimate test of a model. However, a model that best fits the past data may not be the same model that will best fit future data, as was illustrated with the case of the Phillips curve as a forecasting tool. The chapter on methodological individualism argued that one can have more confidence in models built on individualistic foundations to accurately represent future phenomena in the real world.

But in any case, prediction in economics tends to mean the prediction of changes in economic variables. An increase in the price of tea will cause the price and quantity demanded of coffee to increase. An increase in the quantity of money will cause the price level to rise. Note that economic theory does not provide an explanation of why the price of coffee is what it is—except for the non-explanation that it is the result of the tastes and preferences of consumers—nor does economic theory provide an explanation for why the price level is what it is. There are models of money demand that provide a rationale for why people hold money, and therefore why it has some price in terms of other goods, but these models do not explain the price level in the absence of past data on money and the price level. Models of money demand are good for relating changes in factors influencing money demand into changes in the price level, but they do not explain why some price level exists to begin with.

This is not a statement about the way that economic theory has to be, but rather the way it is. Data on the existing quantity of money and the existing price level already exist, so for purposes of prediction, one is most interested in how a change in one factor will cause a change in another factor. Economists have been relatively successful in forecasting of this type, especially considering the relatively imprecise data of the social sciences that are the subject of analysis. But the very nature of economic models makes some types of prediction more accurate than others. The comparative statics methodology used in economics makes economic models more accurate in predicting the direction of change than the amount of a change, and more accurate in predicting the amount of change than the timing of the change.

This can be illustrated with an economic analysis of the rise and decline of the OPEC oil cartel. Applying the standard neoclassical microeconomic analysis to OPEC, the oil industry operated as a competitive industry before 1973, so the price and quantity in the market were the competitive price and quantity. Then the major oil exporters formed a cartel which enabled them to raise the price of oil by restricting the quantity they produced and sold. However, cartels are inherently unstable because each member of the cartel has an incentive to cheat on the cartel agreement. Eventually, the cartel would be unable to control production and the price would fall back to the competitive level.

With hindsight, all of this is perfectly clear and the neoclassical model seems to fit the facts well. It is worth noting that many individuals did not see the energy situation in the 1970s this way,[12] although at least some economists did.[13] But for the present purposes it is interesting to use this example to see what economists can predict accurately and what they cannot. The neoclassical model, with its inherently timeless comparative statics framework, compares hypothetical states of the world rather than changes over time. Actual analysis strictly within the neoclassical model would say that if a cartel existed rather than a competitive market, the cartel price would be higher than the competitive price. And if a cartel existed there would be incentives to cheat on the cartel which would cause it to become a competitive market. The analyst must then be willing to translate this atemporal analysis into a temporal framework and say that the formation of an effective cartel will cause price to rise, but the cartel will eventually disintegrate and price will return to the competitive level.

Here, the neoclassical model predicts accurately, at least within this conveniently chosen example. The direction of change was perfectly forecast, with prices first rising and then falling. Note that the prediction occurs without even appealing to much real-world data. All that was necessary was to know how the structure of the market changed when the cartel formed.

What if one wanted to know the amount of the price changes in addition to the direction of change? Here, the theory needs more help from real-world data. The amount of the price change will depend upon the elasticity of demand in the face of the quantity restriction, and how much the cartel can (or wants to) restrict quantity, which in turn will depend upon the interaction of the marginal cost and demand for oil. These factors can all be estimated. Economists routinely estimate the elasticity of demand for a good, but note that the prediction of the magnitude of the price change will of necessity not be as accurate as the prediction of the direction of the price change. For one thing, the magnitude of the change rests on the same conceptual foundation as the direction, so if the direction is wrong the magnitude will be also, but for another thing, the theory alone predicts the direction of change, whereas the magnitude is something that cannot be estimated without an examination of the real-world data, and whereas the theory would predict the same direction of change no matter what market was affected, the magnitude of the change will depend upon data related specifically to that market.

What if one were also interested in knowing how long it would take for the price to rise, and how long it would remain at the higher level before returning to the initial level? In this case, comparative statics analysis, which was the framework for addressing the first two questions, is of no help whatsoever. The economist could make a guess, but there is no reason to think that the economist's guess would be any better than anyone else's who has studied the problem, for comparative statics, which is a building block of the economic paradigm, does not offer any information about how long it takes for something to happen.

Within the comparative statics framework, the direction of change is a direct implication of the theory, so comparative statics predicts the direction of change better than the amount of change, which requires appeal to the data of the real world.[14] But predicting the amount of time that it will take for the change to occur is outside the realm of comparative statics, and there is no reason to think that the economist will know this any better than anyone else, nor is there any reason to think that someone who has a good track record in predicting the direction of change in economic variables should also be able to predict their timing. The comparative statics nature of economics does not provide the framework.

Economists use models to predict the direction of change, but must use models and data to predict the magnitude of change, and since economic theory provides no help on temporal matters, they must resort to the data alone on timing questions. A forecast amounts to saying that similar things have taken about this long to happen before, so they will probably take about this long to happen again. This may be good information, and can also be accurate. However, economics in its present state provides no theoretical guidelines for how long it takes for economic processes to take their course.

In some matters theory may provide information about how much a variable will change. For example, the quantity theory of money coupled with the distinction between real and nominal magnitudes—both a standard part of the economist's toolbox—will predict that a doubling of the quantity of money will cause a doubling of the price level, all other things held equal. However, this prediction comes within a comparative statics framework, and Milton Friedman's famous dictum about monetary policy is that there are long and variable lags. We can guess how long it will take the effects of monetary policy to trickle through the economy based upon how long it has taken in the past, but the actual length of time it will take is not revealed by the model because the model is a comparative statics model and does not contain a time dimension.

One might want to graft time onto the comparative statics model, but past attempts have not been very fruitful. Perhaps the comparative statics equilibrium models used in economics are not very suited to the task. This is one of the issues that will be taken up in the next chapter; here we only conclude that comparative statics models are good at predicting the direction of change, not as good for predicting the amount of change, and offer no information at all on the amount of time it takes for the change to occur.

CONCLUSION

There is a great deal of diversity in the type of activity that falls under the heading of economics, but the common ground of all economics is that it is based on models. Economics provides insight into the way the world works because the models in economics have a correspondence with the real world phenomena that they model. Models can be useful in providing insight into events of the past, but a model that accurately describes the underlying process of something that happened in the past should also be generalizable to future events that will occur under the same circumstances. The circumstances under which a model will generalize to the future are inherent in the assumptions of the model, even though some assumptions will by necessity be unstated.

The previous chapter looked at methodological individualism as a method for providing some assurance that the conclusions of a model will generalize to future circumstances. Not all models in economics have an individualistic foundation, but it was argued that one can have more confidence in the robustness of results from models that do have this foundation. As such, methodological individualism can be viewed as an important, although not universal, principle of economics.

Individual behavior is usually depicted in economics either by utility functions or demand curves, so these analytical devices are the embodiment of methodological individualism in economics. Even though theorists derive demand curves from utility functions, there is a significant difference between the two types of models. With a demand curve, change always occurs in the direction of the substitution effect, whereas with utility functions there is no a priori way to tell what the result of a particular causal factor will be. Models based on the concepts of supply and demand generally yield unambiguous predictions, whereas when utility functions are the foundation of a model the results will usually be an empirical question.

One of the roles of an economic model is prediction, but models in economics tend to predict changes that will occur as a result of some causal factors rather than predicting an initial state of affairs. Economic models will be useful for predicting changes that result from a shift in relative prices, but are not very useful for understanding why relative prices are what they are in the first place. Economists can try to gain some insight into these issues by seeking explanations for individual behavior in terms of the different relative prices and incomes faced by individuals with identical utility functions. Individuals who live in cold climates will tend to be better hockey players, while those who live in warm climates will tend to be better golfers. But while this will provide some additional insight into individual behavior, it still does not explain the nature of the underlying utility function.

The comparative statics nature of economic models highlights this aspect of economic models. In comparative statics, one hypothetical situation is compared with another, assuming some difference in the two situations. Comparative statics compares the effect of the difference, but assumes (rather than explains) the initial situation.[15] The comparison in comparative statics is timeless in nature, which has implications about the changes that can be forecast using comparative statics. Comparative statics is relatively good at predicting the direction of change in other variables as a result of some change in an initial variable. Comparative statics is not as good at predicting the magnitude of change, and it has nothing to say about the length of time over which the change will occur, since comparative statics is a timeless framework.

The previous chapter looked at the principle of methodological individualism in economic models. This chapter examined the way that methodological individualism is embodied in economic models through demand curves or utility functions, but typically in a static equilibrium framework. The next chapter takes a deeper look into this static equilibrium framework by examining general equilibrium and partial equilibrium as methods of representing economic phenomena in models.

NOTES

1. See Richard B. McKenzie, "The Neoclassicalists vs. the Austrians: A Partial Reconciliation of Competing Worldviews," *Southern Economic Journal* 47, no. 1 (July 1980), pp. 1–13, for a discussion of the Austrian school in this regard.

2. As a point of reference, the classic neoclassical micro theory text by the classic neoclassical economist is C. E. Ferguson, *Microeconomic Theory*, Revised Edition (Homewood, Illinois: Irwin, 1969).

3. Note that income is not a Giffen good unless the individual actually takes home more income after the tax increase than before it.

4. This is not universally accepted as true, however. See James D. Gwartney and Richard Stroup, "Labor Supply and Tax Rates: A Correction of the Record," *American Economic Review* 73, no. 3 (June 1983), pp. 446–51.

5. See Imre Lakatos, *The Methodology of Scientific Research Programmes*, vol. I (Cambridge: Cambridge University Press, 1978), p. 18 and pp. 47–52.

6. Raymond C. Battalio, along with others, has developed a number of economic models of animal behavior. See, for example, Raymond C. Battalio, Leonard Green, and John H. Kagel, "Income-Leisure Tradeoffs of Animal Workers," *American Economic Review* 71, no. 4 (September 1981), pp. 621–32.

7. George J. Stigler and Gary S. Becker, "De Gustibus Non Est Disputandum," *American Economic Review* 67, no. 2 (March 1977), pp. 76–90.

8. Richard B. McKenzie, "The Non-Rational Domain and the Limits of Economic Analysis," *Southern Economic Journal* 46, no. 1 (July 1979), pp. 145–57, presents a dissenting view on this subject.

9. This discussion focuses on the static nature of the model, but perhaps equally significant is the principle of maximization subject to a constraint that drives comparative statics models to an equilibrium. Paul Samuelson, in his Nobel lecture, "Maximum Principles in Analytical Economics," *American Economic Review* 62, no. 3 (June 1972), pp. 249–62, discusses this aspect of comparative statics.

10. See, for example, Israel M. Kirzner, *Competition and Entrepreneurship* (Chicago: University of Chicago Press, 1973). The chapter on utility and entrepreneurship will examine such models in more detail.

11. See Duncan K. Foley and Miguel Sidrauski, *Monetary and Fiscal Policy in a Growing Economy* (New York: Macmillan, 1971), for an elegant neoclassical growth model based on the principles of earlier growth models.

12. See Werner Meyer, "Snake Oil Salesmen," *Policy Review* 37 (Summer 1986), pp. 74–77, for a long series of quotations from prominent individuals, including Kenneth Arrow, that even after the cartel had been established for half a decade, the trend of oil prices would be up, and the quantity trend would be down.

13. See Milton Friedman, "Right at Last, an Expert's Dream," *Newsweek* (March 10, 1986), p. 8, who discusses the oil cartel in terms of the argument used in this section.

14. One can still make money in the market by knowing only the direction of change, even though one could make more if one could also forecast magnitudes of change with equal accuracy.

15. The initial situation may be constructed in order to resemble some real world situation, however.

Chapter 8

EQUILIBRIUM CONCEPTS
IN ECONOMICS

When the only tool you have is a hammer, everything looks like a nail.

Anonymous.

This chapter discusses some aspects of the use of equilibrium concepts in economics. It is not a complete overview of the use of equilibrium models, but rather is an examination of a few issues that arise in the use of equilibrium models. The chapter will begin by looking at the conceptual differences between partial equilibrium and general equilibrium models in economics. The surface differences are readily apparent, as are many similarities. Most obviously, a general equilibrium attempts to model all of the changes that will occur as the result of a certain causal factor. The model is a closed system. With a partial equilibrium analysis, some things not depicted by the model may also be affected by the causal factor. The normal justification for using partial equilibrium models is that factors outside the model will have a negligible impact on the phenomena within the model, and that the user of the model is not interested in phenomena outside the model.

While there are differences between the two types of models, there are also obvious similarities. Both rely on the comparative statics method, and both depict economic phenomena in equilibrium. Furthermore, it is common to construct both types of models from the same basic building blocks of individual behavior. The utility functions and production functions underlying both types of models are often identical. This conveys the impression that a general equilibrium model is just an aggregation of partial equilibrium models of all of the sectors of the economy.

There are differences in the general process of equilibration in each type of model, however, and this chapter will look at the equilibrating process in equilibrium models first. The second major topic of discussion in this chapter is the role of entrepreneurship in equilibrium models. The final topic to be considered is the relationship between equilibrium and economic growth and development. The first step in the discussion of these equilibrium concepts will be to look into the definition of equilibrium.

EQUILIBRIUM IN ECONOMIC MODELS

The concept of equilibrium in economics which at first seems straightforward is in fact viewed in different ways in different types of models. Milton Friedman says, "An equilibrium position is one that if attained will be maintained."[1] This vision of equilibrium, which depicts a situation that is unchanging through time, can be contrasted with the rational expectations view of equilibrium which considers an individual to be in equilibrium if the individual considers himself to be in the optimum position at a point in time, given what he knows at that time.[2] The rational expectations view allows for the possibility that an individual can remain in equilibrium in a changing economy, always adjusting to the changing circumstances as they arise.

There is more than a semantic difference here. These two different concepts of equilibrium depict a different process of economic adjustment over time. Kevin Hoover distinguishes these views by calling the first view the Marshallian view and the second Walrasian.[3] While there is no reason to quarrel with Hoover's terminology, this chapter will later discuss a slightly different concept of general equilibrium that seems more in the spirit of Walras, so will label these concepts Marshallian and new classical, following the name that has been used to describe the rational expectations school of thought.

The Marshallian concept of equilibrium seems most consistent with the comparative statics method that characterizes much of economics. The economy (or a subset) exchanges a certain quantity of goods at certain prices in one static period after another.

Then some change disturbs this equilibrium and some individual or group of individuals find themselves out of equilibrium at the previous period's prices and quantities. For example, in a simple supply and demand framework, something causes the supply curve to shift up and suppliers are no longer willing to supply the same quantity at the old price. When they begin selling less, demanders find themselves unable to purchase all that they want at the old price, and will be willing to pay more. Market forces cause the price to rise as long as suppliers are not in equilibrium, and the price eventually rises to a new higher equilibrium price which is consistent with a lower quantity exchanged.

The adjustment process just described is not in the model; the model shows only the initial and final equilibrium states. That adjustment process seems to be implied, though, and at any rate, if the adjustment does take place, there must be some process like that above that moves the economy from one equilibrium to another. In essence, the process is that some change results in a disequilibrium situation and people adjust their behavior until a new equilibrium is reached.

In the new classical framework, individuals never find themselves out of equilibrium. Rather, given the information they possess, including prices, individuals always adjust immediately to the optimum position. They might adjust differently with more information, of course, but there is no transition through a disequilibrium state on the way to a new equilibrium in the new classical view of the economy. In the Marshallian view, equilibrium is a position toward which the economy is always adjusting. In the new classical view, the economy is always at equilibrium, even though the underlying equilibrium might be changing over time.[4]

Both of these views of equilibrium can be contrasted to a more strictly interpreted Walrasian view of general equilibrium where a vector of prices for all goods is established so that the quantity supplied equals the quantity demanded in all markets. Friedman has argued against the view that Marshall considers a subset of the economy in his partial equilibrium models in economics, as contrasted to the general equilibrium view of Walras.[5] Rather, he argues that Marshall and Walras had fundamentally different notions about how their analyses should be used. For Marshall, economic models were tools for discovering the truth about the real world, whereas for Walras the general equilibrium concept was a formal structure that provided a depiction of all of the economic interdependencies in an economy. But despite these differences between them, both the Walrasian and Marshallian concepts of equilibrium were that of a state of affairs that, once reached, would not change.

In the new classical view, the model of the economy is never in disequilibrium. In the Marshallian and Walrasian views, the economy may be in disequilibrium in transition to the new equilibrium, but any disequilibrium situation will not be a factor in arriving at the new equilibrium. All of these types of models stand in contrast to some models of the economy where disequilibrium is viewed as a significant phenomenon. In some models, trading at disequilibrium prices can cause considerable problems, including the generation of an equilibrium at which some individuals will have excess supplies or demands of various goods at market prices.[6] In other models, the Marshallian disequilibrium adjustment process is the focus of analysis rather than the equilibrium state toward which the economy is tending.[7] As should now be apparent, equilibrium means different things to different economists, and the significance of the concept also varies among economists.

The terms general equilibrium and partial equilibrium also tend to have different connotations to them. While both terms suggest an unchanging state of affairs, partial equilibrium implies that only a subset of the economy is being examined while in general equilibrium, a vector of prices is established so that no individual has any excess demands at that set of prices. If partial equilibrium is thought of in the Marshallian framework as just described, it is possible to imagine a period of disequilibrium during which the market adjusts to new circumstances caused by an exogenous change. In general equilibrium, however, the entire economy is captured by the model, so it is harder to imagine some type of exogenous change that sets in motion an adjustment to a new equilibrium. In fact, there is a general equilibrium conception held by economists where the economy simply remains in this state of equilibrium period after period.

In looking at the concept of equilibrium, then, several distinct views emerge in different models of the economy. The Walrasian general equilibrium is at one end of the continuum. In this conception, the economy is characterized by a steady state equilibrium situation in which all markets clear period after period at equilibrium prices. Close to this is the new classical conception where everyone in the economy remains in equilibrium as the economy adjusts over time. The new classical view differs from the Walrasian view in the amount of information available to traders at any point in time. In the Marshallian view, which is also a general equilibrium view according to Friedman, there may be a period of disequilibrium as the economy adjusts from one equilibrium to another. Perhaps the economy never reaches the equilibrium, but the Marshallian equilibrium is the point toward which the economy is always moving. Then there are disequilibrium views which place more emphasis on the trading at false prices and the resulting problems that can arise that may prevent a Walrasian equilibrium from ever occurring. And there are other models which emphasize the adjustment process rather than the implied equilibrium which is never reached.

These different conceptions of the economy might all have uses, depending on the problem being analyzed. A theme developed earlier in the book was that since models are necessarily simplifications of reality, no model can accurately describe every economic phenomenon, so different models will be appropriate for different purposes. But once a person looks at things in a certain way, it is sometimes hard to see that same thing from other ways, and the concept of equilibrium in economics may have had the effect of channeling economic thought down a certain route without consciously realizing the areas of inquiry that were being overlooked. There is a saying that when the only tool you have is a hammer, everything looks like a nail. Economists steeped in the equilibrium framework may as a result have overlooked some implications of other lines of inquiry. One area where this is almost surely true is in the role of entrepreneurship in economic models.

ENTREPRENEURSHIP AND EQUILIBRIUM

The role of the entrepreneur is well recognized in economics, and entrepreneurship is listed as one of the four factors of production, along with land, labor, and capital, in the typical economics textbook. But after noting the role of entrepreneurship, the textbook discussion of markets then proceeds to examine markets in the static equilibrium framework that is an ingrained part of the economic paradigm. In equilibrium, the role of profits is obscured because profit is the incentive that leads the entrepreneur to allocate resources, but the allocation problem is solved by the time the economy reaches an equilibrium. What is the role of profits in the adjustment process that is left out of all equilibrium models?

There are really two distinctly different views of entrepreneurship in the economics literature. These views can be characterized as Coasian and Knightian after Ronald Coase and Frank Knight, who were both influential in identifying the role of the entrepreneur in the firm.[8] Following this line of reasoning, the two economists had significantly different conceptions about the role that the entrepreneur plays, and these different roles are intimately tied up in the conception of equilibrium implied in the theories.

Coase viewed the economy from a general equilibrium framework. Within this framework there is at first no obvious reason why firms or entrepreneurs should exist at all. Individuals can simply buy anything they desire—including the labor of others—at market prices and allow the invisible hand of the market to take care of resource allocation rather than having an entrepreneur direct the allocation of resources within the firm. Without firms, individuals would contract with each other to exchange for the goods and services that they desire for production and consumption.[9] Coase's explanation for the existence of firms is that there are costs associated with using the price system and these costs must be weighed against the costs of allocating resources from within a firm. Following this line of reasoning, the entrepreneur earns a return for his services by avoiding the costs involved in using the price system, so entrepreneurship becomes a paying proposition when the costs of directly commanding productive resources is lower than purchasing them continually on the market.

One might imagine, for example, the owner of a steel mill trying to contract for labor in the market. Depending on the demand for steel that day, the mill owner might demand a great deal of labor or none at all, and depending upon the market for labor in general, steel workers might be cheap or expensive on any particular day. If labor were contracted for in this way, the laborer would be the residual claimant for the value of labor in the same way that the steel mill owner is the residual claimant for the capital tied up in the mill.

Given the costs involved in trying to contract for labor this way, the mill owner instead can hire labor at an agreed-upon wage regardless of the value of the output produced. This guarantees a steady stream of labor at a predictable price to the mill owner, who has now become an entrepreneur in the steel industry. In Coase's view, firms exist to avoid the costs of using the price mechanism and the entrepreneur decides when there is a gain to be made by avoiding these costs by bringing production inside the firm rather than leaving the exchange relationship in the market.

This Coasian view of entrepreneurship finds itself embodied in much literature on the economics of information.[10] Alchian and Demsetz, for example, model the role of the entrepreneur as one of monitoring employees where shirking is possible.[11] The general idea here is that there are transactions and monitoring costs in the real world and that the return to entrepreneurship is a payment for reducing these costs.[12] This vision of the role of the entrepreneur is tied intimately to the Walrasian view of the economy where there is some optimal general equilibrium allocation of resources that could be produced were it not for the various types of information costs standing in the way. The entrepreneur finds ways to lower these costs and move closer to the optimal general equilibrium allocation of resources, thereby earning a share of economic output.

Knight's concept of the role of the entrepreneur is set on a different foundation. Knight's famous distinction between risk and uncertainty underlies his view of the role of the entrepreneur.[13] In Knight's concept of risk, there are future events that cannot be predicted with certainty, but they fall into a group of events that can be statistically analyzed so that one can predict with some probability about the occurrence of the events. Insurance is based on this notion of risk, for example. While the insurance company cannot predict whether any particular individual will die in some year, or whether any particular individual will be involved in an automobile accident, the probability of these events can be estimated with accuracy given the past behavior of other individuals in similar circumstances. Risk is a quantifiable concept.

With uncertainty, on the other hand, one cannot know ahead of time that any particular event might occur. One might be able to turn uncertainty into risk by pooling a group of similar cases, as the insurance industry does. To use that example again, it is uncertain whether any particular individual will die this year, but by pooling a group of similar individuals and having them all pay premiums, the insurance company can take a measurable risk.

In Knight's conception, the role of the entrepreneur is to take on the uncertainty inherent in future markets, and if the entrepreneur guesses right about the future state of affairs, he will be rewarded with profits. But since market transactions in the future will depend upon many factors that cannot be known ahead of time, and since only one set of circumstances will come to pass, there is genuine uncertainty in decisions about future resource allocation that entrepreneurs must make now. There is uncertainty about future resources and about future productive techniques. But even more, there is uncertainty about the future demands of individuals for final goods and services. If individuals are embodied with the ability to make choices, then their future choices can only be a matter of speculation to the entrepreneur.

The entrepreneur's job is to make decisions now to produce output for future consumption, but the entrepreneur must be uncertain about the future, so must make decisions now based upon partial ignorance. The entrepreneur is compensated for bearing this uncertainty while providing certain returns to the factors of production that he hires. But the return is only earned if the entrepreneur is successful in foreseeing the future.

Note the difference between Knight's view and Coase's view of entrepreneurship. The Coasian entrepreneur is a technician who is skilled at lowering information costs and receives compensation for this skill. The Knightian entrepreneur is compensated for making decisions in the face of uncertainty about the future.

Underlying these different visions of entrepreneurship are the different visions of equilibrium in the economy. In the Coasian view, there is an underlying general equilibrium toward which the economy tends, and the entrepreneur facilitates the movement toward the equilibrium. But recall that static equilibrium models like this are timeless, and in order for the equilibrium concept to work, the general equilibrium in all future periods must be embodied in the present general equilibrium.

The link between the present general equilibrium and the future general equilibrium is current investment that is being made to produce future output. In the Walrasian framework, the equilibrium price vector produces the optimal allocation of resources by making all traders' plans consistent with one another, eliminating such problems as excess demands and trading at false prices. This must imply not only current consumption goods but current investment as well. And since current investment is used to produce future goods, this must also mean that the output of future goods is implied in the present general equilibrium. The implication would be there if there was only one type of investment good, but it is strengthened by the fact that investment goods are heterogeneous. It is difficult to build automobiles in a shoe factory, for example. Thus, today's general equilibrium level of investment in shoe factories is a function of the equilibrium level of shoe production that will take place in the future.

This notion will probably be familiar to economists, who picture a general equilibrium as a steady state situation where one period's production is the same as the previous period's, or perhaps grows at a constant rate. Note that the concept of general equilibrium does not allow for (economic) profits or losses, or trading at what turns out to be a false price. In the real world, one could imagine an individual being overly optimistic about the shoe industry and investing too much in shoe factories, but this is unthinkable in a general equilibrium setting. If mistakes like this could be made, a general equilibrium could not have the qualities of uniqueness and stability that are embodied into the economist's characterization of general equilibrium.

Stated simply, for a general equilibrium to be unique and stable, the Pareto optimal allocation of resources is implied, but for the optimal investment decisions to be made today, tomorrow's general equilibrium must be embodied into today's, and so forth into the future. The timeless general equilibrium really collapses all future resource allocation decisions into the present period. In such a world, there are no Knightian entrepreneurial decisions to be made. The optimal allocation of resources is implied in today's general equilibrium, and the Coasian entrepreneur is an individual who minimizes information and transactions costs and who monitors production in order to move closer to that general equilibrium. The Coasian concept of entrepreneurship follows from a general equilibrium view of the economy.

The Knightian view, in contrast, sees the future vector of demands as characterized by uncertainty. The Knightian entrepreneur guesses at future demands that cannot be known because they are a function of future preferences of individuals, which cannot be known today. Even if one were to try to forecast future preferences, there will be future goods that have never been produced, and since forecasts must come from past data, the information about these future demands cannot be found in the data of the present economy. The essence of entrepreneurship according to Knight, then, is decision making in the face of uncertainty, rather than the reduction of transactions costs and information costs as in the Coasian view. Coase's view follows directly from a general equilibrium conception of the economy, as opposed to the Knightian view that does not see an economy groping for this conceptually identifiable general equilibrium.

The neoclassical framework suggests this Walrasian concept of a stable steady-state equilibrium and most economists are likely to adopt it unconsciously.[14] Even in partial equilibrium analysis, this steady-state general equilibrium notion is implied,[15] so that the market in partial equilibrium is simply viewed as one of the many markets that can be aggregated to produce a general equilibrium. Therefore, the Coasian theory of entrepreneurship is a natural extension of the neoclassical equilibrium framework.

Adopting this framework naturally pushes some questions to the forefront and relegates others to the background. It is natural to look at the characteristics of equilibrium situations, to inquire about complications such as externalities and public goods, or to consider how monetary policy might affect an equilibrium situation. Pushed into the background are questions about how the economy adjusts from one equilibrium to another and whether entrepreneurship and the adjustment process can affect the allocation of resources over the long run. These questions are of little interest in the neoclassical framework since the neoclassical entrepreneur is like a factor of production that facilitates movement toward the underlying equilibrium, rather than being a decision maker under uncertainty that determines how resources will be allocated.[16]

The quotation at the beginning of the chapter, "When the only tool you have is a hammer, everything looks like a nail," finds an analogy here since working within the neoclassical framework makes certain lines of inquiry more readily available than others. The role of entrepreneurship in the economy is a good example. The next section extends this line of inquiry. If the timeless nature of equilibrium models assumes away some important questions, one area worthy of further examination in this light is economic growth and development.

EQUILIBRIUM AND GROWTH

The previous section has set the stage for the theme of this section. Within the neoclassical equilibrium framework there is room for economic growth of only a limited type. The goods to be produced as well as the demands for those goods are taken as given in the model, and as argued earlier, in order for a unique and stable general equilibrium to exist, the setting must be timeless in the sense that all future production and consumption decisions are implied in the present general equilibrium. Otherwise, unique values for investment goods could not be determined within the model, leaving the solution indeterminate.

The neoclassical framework, as a result, leaves much out of the model that can propel economic growth. The parameters of the production functions can change, or inputs into production can be increased. In the neoclassical model, the most obvious opportunity for this to happen lies in the ability of current investment to increase future capital. The neoclassical keys to growth are investment and innovation or technological change, which means a favorable change in the parameters of the production functions.[17]

Economic growth can be visualized in this framework, to be sure, but it obscures more than it illuminates. Why would the coefficients of a production function change over time? One an-swer to this question is perhaps the first lesson in economics, at least if Adam Smith is viewed as the father of economics. Smith began his *Wealth of Nations* by observing how an increase in the division of labor can enhance productivity. Recall Smith's pin fac-tory, where some individuals specialized in drawing the wire for the pins while others specialized in sharpening the ends, and so forth, could produce more pins collectively than if each one spent the same amount of time manufacturing entire pins. Therefore, productivity is enhanced by dividing the production process into smaller and smaller subtasks to take advantage of the increased productivity of the division of labor.

Following this line of reasoning, the average cost of production can be brought ever lower by increased specialization and divi-sion of labor. The process of specialization cannot go on forever, though, because, as Adam Smith noted, the division of labor is limited by the extent of the market.[18] Simply following along with Smith's insight illuminates the process of economic growth that has occurred in the past several centuries. Markets can be extended in two ways. They can be extended geographically, or they can be extended by increasing the wealth of individuals in a given geographical area to provide them with more income and therefore a bigger market for output. In Britain in Adam Smith's day, for example, the increasing productivity of Britain provided its citizens with more income and therefore provided a bigger market for British manufacturing output.[19] In the United States, economic growth surpassed that of Europe because of the larger market unimpeded by trade barriers among the many European nations. The development of navigable waterways, then railways, then interstate highways, further served to extend the markets that could be served, for final products as well as intermediate goods. The development of the Japanese and Korean economies since World War II have been heavily dependent upon extend-ing the market for their products well beyond their shores. These examples serve to illustrate the point.

From a methodological standpoint, there are some interesting implications inherent in this line of analysis. The whole notion of increasing productivity due to increasing specialization im-plies a decreasing long-run average cost of production.[20] Yet the neoclassical model of competitive equilibrium is built upon the foundation of the equality of average and marginal costs in equilibrium. Increasing returns to scale leads to monopoly in the neoclassical model, and when a single price is charged for a good, prevents the equality of price and marginal cost which is necessary for optimality in the comparative static model.

Despite these difficulties in incorporating the notion of increasing returns due to specialization into equilibrium models, the concept of increasing returns does seem to be a plausible engine for economic growth. Consider a simple example. One would not build a hammer if there was only one nail to be hammered, but would get by with some other implement. Only if a sufficient amount of construction is taking place will it be worthwhile to have individuals specialize in making hammers. Likewise, specialization in the British textile industry in the 1700s and assembly line production in the American automobile industry in the 1900s occurred after a sufficient market materialized to make these techniques worthwhile.

Throughout the book, one theme has been that different models will be appropriate for different purposes. This section suggests that the general equilibrium framework is not a good one for analyzing economic growth because it assumes away some important factors in economic growth. Economists have used the general equilibrium framework anyway, at least in part because it is hard to see the world in some other way once one has established a certain vision of the world. An alternative foundation has been suggested here, based on specialization and the division of labor, but this foundation by itself is not a model of growth and development. Can one be developed along these lines? It is a possible area of inquiry, and an exploration of some of the methodological foundations points the way and also illuminates some of the difficulties in integrating models of specialization and the division of labor with neoclassical equilibrium models. In the neoclassical models, the goods to be produced and techniques used to produce them are taken as given. Many elements of growth and development are therefore assumed away.

The notion of entrepreneurship explored in the last section can be illuminated a bit more here in closing this section. In the neoclassical setting, an entrepreneur is a factor of production that reduces information and transactions costs in aiming at an underlying equilibrium. The Knightian conception of entrepreneurship casts the entrepreneur as a decision maker under uncertainty. The nature of those decisions and of the uncertainty faced by the entrepreneur can be illuminated by seeing increasing returns as the engine of growth. Average costs of production can always be lowered by increasing specialization, but this means a larger quantity of output. An important entrepreneurial decision is to judge the extent of the market to decide if larger scale production at lower prices can be justified by the extent of the market. The successful entrepreneur initiates a more specialized production process at the optimal time.

CONCLUSION

This chapter has covered a number of topics relating to the use of equilibrium in economics. The concept of equilibrium is firmly ingrained into the contemporary paradigm in economics. In the comparative statics method that characterizes the bulk of economics, equilibrium settings are examined in a timeless setting, and although economists talk about adjustment from one equilibrium to another, this adjustment process is left out of the economic models themselves.

There are a number of different ways that economists approach the idea of equilibrium in economics. At one extreme is the Walrasian general equilibrium which is a steady-state situation in which a price vector exists which clears all markets at all times. As argued above, a general equilibrium at one point in time implies general equilibrium at all future times as well. Close to this view of equilibrium is the new classical view that models all individuals as being in individual equilibrium at every point in time, given the information available to that individual. This contrasts with the Marshallian view in which there is a period of disequilibrium between equilibriums, and the disequilibrium setting provides the incentives for economic actors to take actions that move the economy toward equilibrium. At the opposite end of the spectrum from the Walrasian view are economists who find the greatest insight into the operation of the economy to be in the process of adjustment toward equilibrium. In a constantly changing world, a stable equilibrium can never be maintained, so this view contends that the economy cannot be understood without understanding the underlying adjustment process.

The concept of an underlying general equilibrium in an economy affects the way that economists approach certain problems. The quotation at the beginning of the chapter, "When the only tool you have is a hammer, everything looks like a nail," is appropriate here. This chapter looked at two such problems: the role of the entrepreneur, and the concept of economic growth.

Since there is an underlying equilibrium in the equilibrium view of the economy, the role of the entrepreneur in this view is to move the economy toward this equilibrium. This makes the entrepreneur a factor of production that lowers transactions and information costs. By characterizing the future of the economy as uncertain, the entrepreneur takes on another role of a different character. In this alternative approach, the entrepreneur makes decisions under uncertainty and determines by those decisions how resources are to be allocated. In the equilibrium view, resource allocation is determined by the underlying utility and production functions in the economy. In the alternative approach, future resource allocation is uncertain.

This notion can be extended by looking at the process of economic growth and development. Again, the equilibrium approach takes the underlying production functions to be given, whereas the application of Adam Smith's first lesson of economics on the division of labor implies that the economy is characterized by increasing returns, and that economic progress occurs by enlarging markets in order to take advantage of a greater division of labor.

One cannot argue with the success of the neoclassical paradigm in economics, so this analysis is not meant to imply that this model should be discarded. But a persistent theme of this book has been that an economic model, because it is a simplification of reality, cannot be expected to be appropriate for modeling all economic phenomena. Different models will be appropriate for different purposes. By examining the underlying assumptions of equilibrium models, it appears that significant insight is lost in using those models to represent the processes of entrepreneurship and economic growth. But while this points the way toward promising areas of research in economic theory, promises are not results, and the neoclassical theories in these areas will have to stand until better alternatives present themselves.

In the area of entrepreneurship there are some alternatives, and the next chapter applies some of the methodological principles from earlier chapters to models of utility and entrepreneurship.

NOTES

1. Milton Friedman, *Price Theory: A Provisional Text*, Revised Edition (Chicago: Aldine, 1962), p. 19.

2. See Robert E. Lucas, "Understanding Business Cycles," in Karl Brunner and Alan H. Meltzer, eds., *Stabilization of the Domestic and International Economy* (Amsterdam: North Holland, 1977), pp. 7–30.

3. Kevin D. Hoover, "Two Types of Monetarism," *Journal of Economic Literature* 22, no. 1 (March 1984), pp. 58–76.

4. It is interesting to note that Robert Lucas finds Freidrich Hayek to be an intellectual antecedent in this work, linking his current work with Hayek's work decades before. He quotes Hayek's *Monetary Theory and the Trade Cycle* (New York: Augustus M. Kelly, 1966 [orig. 1933]) in this regard in his "Understanding Business Cycles," in *Studies in Business Cycle Theory* (Cambridge: MIT Press, 1981), pp. 215–39. Present day members of the Austrian school see important distinctions between the rational expectations school and the Austrian trade cycle theory, however. See William N. Butos, "Hayek and General Equilibrium Analysis," *Southern Economic Journal* 52, no. 2 (October 1985), pp. 332–43.

5. See Milton Friedman, "The Marshallian Demand Curve," *Journal of Political Economy* 57, no. 6 (December 1949), pp. 463–95.

6. Perhaps the most prominent of this type of theory was promoted by Clower's dual decision hypothesis. See Robert W. Clower, "The Keynesian Counter-Revolution: A Theoretical Appraisal," chapter 19, in R. W. Clower, ed., *Monetary Theory* (Baltimore: Penguin, 1969), and also Axel Leijonhufvud, *On Keynesian Economics and the Economics of Keynes* (London: Oxford University Press, 1968).

7. See Israel M. Kirzner, *Competition and Entrepreneurship* (Chicago: University of Chicago Press, 1973) for an example.

8. See Donald J. Boudreaux and Randall G. Holcombe, "The Coasian and Knightian Theories of the Firm," *Managerial and Decision Economics* (forthcoming).

9. See Ronald H. Coase, "The Nature of the Firm," in George J. Stigler and Kenneth E. Boulding, *Readings in Price Theory* (Chicago: Richard D. Irwin, 1952), pp. 331–51.

10. The seminal article in this literature is George J. Stigler, "The Economics of Information," *Journal of Political Economy* 69 (June 1961), pp. 213–25.

11. Armen A. Alchian and Harold Demsetz, "Production, Information Costs, and Economic Organization," *American Economic Review* 62 (December 1972), pp. 777–95.

12. Also related is the notion of agency costs in the theory of the firm promoted by Michael Jensen and William Meckling, "The Theory of the Firm: Managerial Behavior, Agency Costs, and Ownership Structure," *Journal of Financial Economics* 3 (October 1976), pp. 305–60.

13. See Frank H. Knight's *Risk, Uncertainty, and Profit* (Boston: Houghton Mifflin, 1921) and "Profits and Entrepreneurial Functions," *Journal of Economic History*, vol. 2 supplement (December 1942), pp. 126–32.

14. See Randall G. Holcombe, "Concepts of Public Sector Equilibrium," *National Tax Journal* 33, no. 1 (March 1980), pp. 77–88, where the author implies this Coasian steady-state general equilibrium framework rather than the Knightian alternative, since this is how the literature has developed.

15. See, for example, Milton Friedman, "The Marshallian Demand Curve," cited above.

16. Israel Kirzner's *Competition and Entrepreneurship*, cited earlier, is an example of an alternative conception of the competitive process. See also Gerald P. O'Driscoll Jr., and Mario J. Rizzo, *The Economics of Time and Ignorance* (Oxford: Basil Blackwell Ltd., 1985), for a related discussion.

17. See John R. Hicks, "The Mainspring of Economic Growth," *American Economic Review* 71, no. 6 (December 1981), pp. 23–29, for an example of a discussion of economic growth within this neoclassical framework.

18. See George J. Stigler, "The Division of Labor is Limited by the Extent of the Market," *Journal of Political Economy* (June 1951), pp. 185–93, reprinted in William Breit and Harold M. Hochman, eds., *Readings in Microeconomics*, 2d ed. (New York: Holt, Rinehart, and Winston, 1971), pp. 140–48, for a development of this theme in a neoclassical setting.

19. Nicholas Kaldor, "The Irrelevance of Equilibrium Economics," *Economic Journal* 82 (December 1972), pp. 1237–55, relates this idea to the Keynesian multiplier theory.

20. See Piero Sraffa, "The Laws of Returns Under Competitive Conditions," *Economic Journal* 36 (December 1926), pp. 535–50, and, more significantly, Allyn A. Young, "Increasing Returns and Economic Progress," *Economic Journal* 38 (December 1928), pp. 527–42, for a discussion of these ideas earlier in the 20th century.

Chapter 9

THEORIES OF UTILITY AND ENTREPRENEURSHIP

> But economic theory must be more than a structure of tautologies if it is to be able to predict and not merely describe the consequences of action. . . .
>
> Milton Friedman (1953, pp. 11–12).

The common ground of all modern economics is the reliance on models as the starting point for economic analysis. Because any model assumes away some characteristics of the real world, no model will be appropriate for all purposes. This chapter will compare the Austrian and neoclassical theories of utility and entrepreneurship. One purpose of this comparison is to illustrate how different models will be appropriate for different purposes, even when analyzing the same phenomena. Another purpose is to illustrate that the way one looks at the world defines the interesting issues and relevant questions for further inquiry. As such, the chapter serves as a case study to illustrate the importance of methodological issues in economic inquiry. While one need not be concerned in great detail about one's methodology (as long as one follows the models accepted in the profession), methodological foundations are nevertheless important determinants of the conclusions one reaches, and even of the issues one deems worthy of study.

The chapter uses the Austrian and neoclassical models as elements of analysis, and it is worth noting at the outset that each of these schools of thought has many members, so it is obvious that some economists who consider their ideas to be a part of one of these schools may object to the characterization of their schools' ideas presented here. Recognizing this, the chapter will not try to argue that the characterizations presented here are the true neo-classical or Austrian theories, but rather that they are theories that are widely (but not unanimously) held by those traditions. The main focus of the argument will be on when the theories admit the possibility that individuals might not behave as the theory predicts. Both theories characterize individuals as utility maximizers and entrepreneurs as profit maximizers, so this provides a common framework for discussion. Differences arise because the Austrian theory considers utility maximization to be axiomatic, while the neoclassical theory allows for cases where utility is not being maximized. In contrast, the neoclassical theory takes profit maximization to be axiomatic, while the Austrian theory allows for cases where profit is not maximized.

These differences are related to more general methodological differences between the neoclassical and Austrian schools of thought. Neoclassical economics has developed in a manner that generates testable implications of the theory, but many Austrians hold the view that knowledge in economics arises from deductive reasoning, and that empirical tests are not a proper part of economics.[1] It will be argued below that the differences in the Austrian and neoclassical theories of utility and entrepreneurship are directly related to the question of empirical testability. Specifically, in both cases the neoclassical theory is designed to produce testable implications, whereas the Austrian theory is not. The differences are directly related to the earlier discussion on the intended uses of economic models. The intended uses of the models will be discussed following a comparison of consumer behavior and entrepreneurship.

UTILITY THEORY AND CONSUMER BEHAVIOR

The Austrian theory of utility and consumer behavior is probably best characterized by the writings of Ludwig von Mises, in *Human Action*.[2] As characterized by Mises, human action is always rational because an individual, when faced with choices, always chooses the alternative that appears at the time to best promote the individual's goals. An outside observer with more information, or even the individual chooser through hindsight, may come to view a choice as not being the best one, but this does not contradict the fact that at the time the choice is made, the individual chooser views the option to be taken to be the best one available. It is worth quoting Mises to get a flavor of this argument.

Human action is necessarily always rational. The term "rational action" is pleonastic and must be rejected as such. When applied to the ultimate ends of action, the terms rational and irrational are inappropriate and meaningless. The ultimate end of action is always the satisfaction of some desires of the acting man. . . . No man is qualified to declare what would make another man happier or less discontented. (p. 19)

In the Austrian tradition, the utility maximizing option is defined as the option chosen, so that human action by definition is utility maximizing. Rothbard, in *Man, Economy, and State*[3] provides a good example.

suppose that a man, Jones, chooses each of two alternatives A and B about fifty percent of the time, upon repeated opportunities. This shifting is alleged to be a demonstration that Jones is really indifferent between the two alternatives. Yet what is the reasonable inference? Clearly, that in some cases, A was preferred to B on Jones' value scale, and that in the others, the positions were shifted so that B was preferred to A. In no case was there indifference between the two alternatives. The shift in choice indicates a shift in the preference scale, and not indifference on a constant scale. (p. 268)

These quotations display the general flavor of the Austrian model of consumer behavior.[4] It is axiomatic that consumers act in order to maximize utility. Any choice is by definition rational so that it is not possible to observe behavior that is not utility maximizing. Both Mises and Rothbard recognize the possibility that without perfect knowledge, a choice which appeared to be optimal at the time it was made may later be regretted. Rothbard (p. 6) says, "The omnipresence of uncertainty introduces the ever-present possibility of *error* in human action. The actor may find, after he has completed his action, that the means have been inappropriate to the attainment of his end." And Mises notes (p.

20), "An action unsuited to the end sought falls short of expectations. It is contrary to purpose, but it is rational, i.e., the outcome
of a reasonable—although faulty—deliberation and attempt—although an ineffectual attempt—to obtain a definite goal." Even
here, though, behavior is rational and utility maximizing, given
the information possessed by the individual. The Austrian theory
holds utility maximization as an axiom of human behavior. Behavior that is not utility maximizing is not possible, according to
the Austrian theory.[5]

The Austrian theory seems eminently reasonable as a description of human behavior. Why would an individual act except to
further his or her goals? Yet the neoclassical theory goes a step
further in specifying a preference function that makes assumptions about the types of choices that an individual will make in
order to maximize utility. The authority to be used here on the
neoclassical theory will be Ferguson's *Microeconomic Theory*, Revised Edition.[6] This choice appears to be appropriate because the
late Professor Ferguson seems to qualify as the prototypical neoclassical economist. As with the Austrian theory, however, there
will be those who consider themselves in the neoclassical tradition, but will object to the characterization of neoclassical utility
theory made here.

According to Ferguson (pp. 12–14), the individual's preference
function has the following characteristics. It can rank-order every
conceivable bundle of commodities. Rankings must be commuta-
tive and transitive. Individuals always prefer more to less. Furthermore, "Each consumer has exact and full knowledge of all
information relevant to his consumption decisions. . ." (p. 14).[7]
These assumptions are made in the neoclassical tradition not because they have to be true, but because, although they seem to
be generally reasonable, they may be false. This gives the neoclassical theory predictive content that is absent in the Austrian
theory.

To see the difference in the theories, consider some examples.
First, an economics professor at one university is offered a similar job at a similar university, but at twice the professor's current
salary. Will the professor accept the offer? The neoclassical theory predicts that the offer will be accepted, since more is preferred
to less. The Austrian theory makes no prediction, but does assert

that whichever option is taken will maximize the utility of the chooser. Second, a traveler exits an interstate highway to purchase gasoline. Two gas stations are beside each other, with one offering a gas price 5 cents per gallon less than the other. At which station will the motorist refuel? The neoclassical theory predicts the cheaper one. The Austrian theory cannot predict which will be chosen, but does assert that whichever option is chosen will maximize the utility of the chooser.

The Austrian utility theory is devoid of predictive content due to its assumption that individuals always choose the utility maximizing option, while the neoclassical theory goes a step further to specify general characteristics of utility maximizing behavior that allow it to predict which option will be chosen. The predictive power of the neoclassical theory can be seen when the professor moves and the motorist buys the inexpensive gasoline, but what happens when the professor declines the offer and the motorist buys the expensive gasoline? In this case, it seems that neoclassical economists accept a part of the Austrian tradition rather than claim that utility theory has been falsified. The neoclassical economist may seek more information and discover that the professor did not like the part of the country where the new job would be located, or that the professor's children wanted to remain at their present secondary school. They may find that the motorist preferred the brand name of the more expensive gasoline, or that the motorist did not even notice the price difference. Thus, taking these additional factors into account, utility theory is true after all.

Rationalizations like this illustrate what Lakatos has called the protective belt of assumptions that surround a theory and prevent it from being falsified by an empirical test. Chapter 5 on positivism noted that because the theory itself is protected by assumptions in this way, empirical testing of a theory cannot occur.

Of course, if these other factors had been taken into account before the fact, a different prediction might have emerged from the neoclassical theory, but the possibility still exists that the prediction would be wrong. The simple fact is that when a theory of human behavior predicts that one of a set of possible outcomes will occur, the possibility always exists that the prediction will be wrong. Rather than abandon the neoclassical theory, neoclassicists tend to borrow some Austrianism and claim that if only more information were available, it would be evident that the individual in question was really acting in a manner that the individual believed was utility maximizing at the time. Despite neoclassical rhetoric, it appears that neoclassical economists do not accept the possibility that individuals act contrary to their self-interests.

A neoclassical defense of the additional postulates of utility maximizing might be that most of the time, people act as the additional postulates predict. Neoclassical economics is a powerful predictor, so the neoclassicist is willing to accept the fact that some people will violate the postulates of utility maximization at some times, in exchange for a theory with predictive content. The Austrian, on the other hand, is unwilling to accept a theory of human behavior in which cases arise that violate the postulates of the theory. This discussion relates directly to the discussion earlier in the book about the intended purposes of a model. The connection will be addressed later in the chapter.

The bottom line is that both the Austrian and neoclassical theories of consumer behavior state that the consumer acts to maximize utility. The theory is modeled differently by each school, however. In the Austrian theory, the consumer must by definition act to maximize utility. Since any action is consistent with utility maximization in the Austrian view, the theory has no predictive content, and no testable implications. It is only descriptive. The neoclassical theory, by describing utility maximizing behavior, has predictive content and testable implications. The neoclassical theory also allows the possibility that consumers may act in a manner that is not utility maximizing.

THEORIES OF ENTREPRENEURSHIP

Both Austrian and neoclassical theories of individual behavior begin with the assumption that individuals maximize utility. Likewise, both theories of entrepreneurship assume that entrepreneurs maximize profit. At this point, the theories diverge. The neoclassical theory takes profit maximizing behavior to be axiomatic, whereas the Austrian theory recognizes that while profits are the goal of the entrepreneur, entrepreneurs might fail to pursue some profit enhancing activity. The discussion in this section will begin with the Austrian theory.

Perhaps the most explicit account of the Austrian theory of entrepreneurship is Israel Kirzner's *Competition and Entrepreneurship*.[8] Kirzner argues that while the goal of the entrepreneur is profit maximization, more is necessary than the simple calculation of which is the most profitable of the several alternatives known to the entrepreneur. What entrepreneurial activity really consists of is an alertness to recognize unexploited profit opportunities. "For each product, as well as for each resource, opportunities for mutually beneficial exchange among potential buyers and sellers are missed. The potential sellers are unaware that sufficiently eager buyers are waiting, who might make it worth their while to sell." (pp. 69–70). Thus, individuals who are trying to maximize profits miss some potential profit opportunities, and so are not in fact maximizing profits because of the unexploited opportunities. Entrepreneurship is the discovery of these unexploited opportunities.

The Austrian theory of entrepreneurship is couched in this framework because the Austrians seek to explain the process by which the market tends toward equilibrium, rather than the characteristics of the equilibrium which, because the economy is constantly changing, cannot be reached.[9] The methodology that the Austrians use for this purpose characterizes entrepreneurs as striving to maximize profits, but falling short of the goal because new profit opportunities are continually arising. Thus, there is always room for more entrepreneurship.[10] In the Austrian theory, firms have the goal of profit maximization, but they may not actually achieve this goal.

In the neoclassical theory, by contrast, firms are assumed to be profit maximizers, and unlike the Austrian theory, the neoclassical theory does not allow for the possibility that firms do not maximize profits. Ferguson (p. 221) nicely sums up the neoclassical position when he says ". . .entrepreneurs try to maximize profit." This statement is followed by a footnote: "For the purpose of *explaining* business behavior it is sufficient to assume that entrepreneurs act *as if* they tried to maximize profit. For the purpose of predicting business behavior the *as if* assumption is the only justifiable one." Ferguson's text continues by arguing:

Whether profit maximization is a reasonable assumption is a question long debated in economics. Several important criticisms have been brought to bear. However, these criticisms do not overcome the fact that the assumption of profit maximization is the only one providing a general theory of firms, markets, and resource allocation that is successful both in explaining and predicting business behavior.

On the same page, Ferguson readily admits that ". . . not all producers try to maximize profits at all times." This is even stronger than the Austrian position that entrepreneurs may not always be successful at their attempts, yet Ferguson still argues that profit maximization is a necessary assumption, even if it is sometimes contrary to fact.[11] Only by using the assumption does the theory have testable implications and predictive content. The Austrian theory, by contrast, admits any type of behavior by firms and by entrepreneurs, because although firms try to maximize profits, the entrepreneur may not have observed, for examples, a profitable opportunity to change a price or enter a new market.

The Austrian argument could be taken a step further, to utility theory. The entrepreneur is an individual who may have goals other than profit maximization, and so may engage in behavior that is not profit maximizing to further these other goals. But while this step is possible, it is not necessary to the current argument, since the entrepreneur in Austrian theory may simply fail to observe a profit opportunity. With entrepreneurs being allowed within the theory to fail to capitalize on profitable opportunities, the Austrian theory is consistent with any behavior of the firm and the entrepreneur. As a result, the Austrian theory does not contain testable implications, nor does it have predictive content. A well-known example of the application of neoclassical micro theory is the article by Averch and Johnson, "Behavior of the Firm under Regulatory Constraint." [12] They argue that when a firm is regulated to earn a specific rate of return on capital, the firm will respond by becoming more capital intensive, which will earn it more profit. Subsequent work empirically verified their theory. The Austrian theory is consistent with their theory, but would also be consistent with the opposite finding, since the entrepreneur may not have observed the profit opportunity. Furthermore, the entrepreneur in a regulated industry will be sheltered from competition, thus lowering the incentive to exploit the opportunity. The Austrian theory is consistent with both outcomes, while the neoclassical theory predicts one.

In summary, the Austrian and neoclassical theories both begin with profit maximizing entrepreneurs, but while the neoclassical theory takes profit maximization to be axiomatic, and does not allow for the possibility of non-profit maximizing behavior, the Austrian theory leaves open the possibility that entrepreneurs may pursue activities that are in fact not profit maximizing. As a result of this difference, the Austrian theory is consistent with any market outcome, and has no predictive content or testable implications. The neoclassical theory, by using the restrictive assumption of profit maximization as an axiom, does have testable implications and predictive content. A fuller contrast between the two theories will be drawn in the next section.

AUSTRIAN AND NEOCLASSICAL THEORIES

The two preceding sections have developed an interesting contrast. Both schools of thought ascribe utility maximization and profit maximization as the goals of consumers and entrepreneurs. However, the Austrian theory holds utility maximization to be axiomatic, while entrepreneurs may fail to maximize profit as described by the theory. Neoclassical theory, on the other hand, allows the possibility that consumers may fail to maximize utility as described by the theory, while profit maximization by entrepreneurs is axiomatic. Austrians take utility maximization to be axiomatic, but not profit maximization, while neoclassicists take profit maximization to be axiomatic, but not utility maximization.

This curious contrast in the cases where economic actors axiomatically must behave according to the theory and where the theory allows them to deviate from their goals is consistent with the larger views of both schools on issues that extend well beyond the theories of utility and entrepreneurship. The issues of descriptive and predictive abilities of models have already been mentioned. The neoclassical model is constructed in order to give it as much predictive ability as possible, and the assumptions are chosen for that purpose. The Austrian model is designed more to describe and understand the process by which the economy operates, and the Austrian view is that economic truths are logically deduced from economic principles. Given the validity of the first principles, knowledge gained by logical deduction must be true, and empirical testing of the validity of a theory is neither necessary nor desirable.

The antiempirical stance taken by many Austrian economists is quite consistent with the Austrian theories of utility and entrepreneurship. Those theories are designed in order to eliminate any empirical content. The theories are consistent with any state of the world. This is not because the Austrians want a theory that is devoid of any empirical content; it is because the goal of economic theory as seen by the Austrians is to understand the market process that leads from disequilibrium to equilibrium. In order for this process to occur, something unpredicted must have occurred to produce a disequilibrium, and the necessary steps toward equilibrium must be uncertain as well. In the move toward equilibrium, the activities of a multitude of market participants must somehow be coordinated, and it is the coordinating process that is of interest to the Austrians. The result has been a theory without predictive ability or testable implications. With this view of economics, it is evident why Austrians tend to view empirical work in economics as overemphasized. In the Austrian view, empirical work is useful to discover historical relationships among economic variables, but never can empirical work be used to test a theory.

The Austrian models that depict the market process can be contrasted with the neoclassical models that describe the economy in equilibrium, with predictable characteristics that result from economic activity. The predictable characteristics described by the models naturally point toward the possibility of empirical work to see whether the predictable characteristics of the models manifest themselves in the real world. Testing the models against past events suggests the possibility of using the models to predict future events. Some models will predict better than others, of course. These issues were discussed earlier. However, models with predictable characteristics ought to be describing a world with predictable characteristics as well.

EMPIRICAL AND THEORETICAL APPROACHES TO ECONOMICS

The Misesian approach to economic theory regards utility maximization as axiomatic, and then wants to logically deduce a body of economic theory. This extreme view can be contrasted with the equally extreme view that all questions are empirical questions, and that theory cannot deduce anything about the real world. In the middle lies the neoclassical view which accepts certain axioms of behavior, like wealth maximization in individuals and profit maximization in firms, but leaves other elements of economics in the domain of empirical questions. The brief argument here is that the Misesian view and the extreme empirical view are in fact closely allied. A theory that allows for any type of behavior really must appeal to the data to know what will happen in the real world. With Misesian utility maximizers and Kirznerian entrepreneurs, any outcome is possible, and only through observation of the real world can the actual outcome be discovered. This is closely allied with the extreme empiricist view that all economic questions are empirical questions.

These views are at odds with the neoclassical approach that takes some specific actions as axiomatic. Both of the above views would find fault with the neoclassical axioms; the Austrians because the axioms do not allow for the full range of economic behavior, which is a faulty heuristic assumption; the empiricists because the assumptions are sometimes false, a faulty domain assumption. The point is, however, that the Austrian methodological position is very close to the empiricist view that all economic questions are empirical questions, at least in some respects, and that both find fault with the neoclassical view that axiomatically eliminates some types of human action from the domain of economic theory.

MODELS AND METHODOLOGY

Earlier in the book, models were viewed as analogies to real-world economic phenomena. Economic models are simpler than the real world, and it was argued that they had to be. When faced with a choice of models, the question of which is the best model arises. The answer given earlier was that different models would be appropriate for different tasks, so that there really is no such thing as a best model for all purposes. Models are necessarily simplifications of the real world, and the best model for a particular purpose may leave out some important elements for another purpose.

These conclusions about economic models can be applied to the differences in Austrian and neoclassical models just discussed. The differences appear to be methodological, regarding assumptions and, indeed, methods of economic research. But viewed within the framework developed earlier in the book, the differences narrow to the question of selecting the appropriate model for the purpose at hand. One who views the purpose of economic analysis as understanding the operation of market processes will favor the Austrian view, whereas one interested in predicting economic phenomena will favor the neoclassical.

The views presented here of the Austrian and neoclassical schools agree more with the written work of economists of both schools than with their ideas in conversation.[13] This was alluded to before. Austrians seem as quick as any economists to predict the consequences of particular laws, regulations, or technological developments. Predictably, the Austrians' predictions are based upon assumptions of wealth maximizing individuals and profit maximizing businesses. Any outcome is consistent with the Austrian model, but Austrians tend to use the neoclassical model to decide what is most likely.

A similar observation applies to neoclassical economists. A finding of an upward sloping demand curve will be taken as a reason to reject the empirical work rather than the law of demand.

A neoclassical economist who discovers non-wealth maximizing behavior will not reject utility theory, but will search for additional variables until the empirical evidence agrees with the theory. Although neoclassical economists claim that their models are empirically falsifiable, in reality they consider—in the Austrian tradition—that the theory is always correct. A contradiction in the theory prompts the researcher to search for additional evidence. The search continues until the evidence agrees with the theory, at which time the research is finished.[14] This methodology, which is used much more than it is described, is essentially Austrian. The neoclassical economist, while claiming that utility theory is potentially falsifiable, will never accept evidence that the theory is contradicted.

The divergence between the neoclassical and Austrian views on methodology and model building is not as great as it first appears. The divergence seems to be relatively large in the written works of each group, but it seems that each group has adopted many of the ideas of the other in their thinking about economic problems and methodology. The reason relates to the discussion on models earlier in the book. Different models will be most appropriate in different circumstances. For predicting the consequences of specified actions, the model must make assumptions about behavior that restrict the possible outcomes of the model. This implies assumptions that restrict the possible choices of individuals within the model. A neoclassical perspective is implied. On the other hand, to understand why individuals act as they do in specific situations, the model that offers complete understanding must allow for any possible outcome. The Austrian perspective is used here. The appropriate model depends on the purpose for which it is to be used.

CONCLUSION

James Buchanan closed an article on methodology with the statement, "Concentration on methodology won't solve any of the problems for you, but at least you should know what the problems are."[15] Buchanan's statement suggests that the methodological distinctions discussed in this chapter will solve no problems. Indeed, if it contains a lesson, it is that economists should not concern themselves over methodological differences with their peers. Different methods will be appropriate for different types of problems, and the distinctions among the methods of various schools of economics may simply reflect the different types of problems that the schools are interested in examining. This would seem to allude to Samuelson's statement quoted at the beginning of the first chapter about methodological prattle. The answer is not quite this simple, however, and there are some important methodological issues that go beyond simply choosing the right model for the task at hand.

The chapter will conclude by mentioning some of those issues, if not resolving them. A key argument has been that often differences in methodology result from the different intended purposes of the models. A model intended to convey a general understanding of economic activity will rest on a different foundation from one intended to make specific predictions. This argument, if accepted, will make economists of different schools of thought more tolerant of methodological differences. However, the model does not imply that every model will be most appropriate for some purpose. In economics, and in any science dealing with human behavior, the realism of assumptions is important to the accuracy of the model. In order to judge the appropriateness of the assumptions, models should find their foundations in the behavior of individuals, rather than aggregates. Inappropriate assumptions could still be made, but the researcher will have a much greater chance of selecting assumptions that are restrictive enough to give the level of prediction desired without eliminating the forces that are likely to be relevant in the real world if the model adheres to the tenets of methodological individualism.

Both the Austrian and the neoclassical theories discussed in this chapter rest on individualistic foundations, despite their differences. In looking at the differences between the Austrian and neoclassical theories of utility and entrepreneurship, it was noted that utility maximization is axiomatic to the Austrians but profit maximization is not, whereas profit maximization is axiomatic to the neoclassicals but utility maximization is not. This distinction was related to the way in which both theories relate to empirical phenomena in the real world. The Austrian models are more suited to explaining while the neoclassical models are more suited to predicting.

This suggests a host of additional issues regarding empirical work and its role in economics, since the ultimate differences in the theories trace their roots back to the relationship between the model and real-world phenomena. The next chapter picks up at this point and provides a discussion of empirical work in economics.

NOTES

1. See Mario J. Rizzo, "Praxeology and Econometrics: A Critique of Positivist Economics," in Louis M. Spadaro, ed., *New Directions in Austrian Economics* (Kansas City: Sheed Andrews and McMeel, Inc., 1978), on this point.

2. Ludwig von Mises, *Human Action: A Treatise on Economics*, 3d rev. ed. (Chicago: Henry Regnery Company, 1966).

3. Murray N. Rothbard, *Man, Economy, and State* (Los Angeles: Nash, 1962).

4. Note the distinction between the theory and the model here. The theory is utility maximization, but the model depicts any action as utility maximizing.

5. Note the similarity here between the Austrian school and the new classical school discussed in the previous chapter.

6. C. E. Ferguson, *Microeconomic Theory*, Revised Edition (Homewood, Illinois: Irwin, 1969).

7. The reader might object to this assumption, citing the work of Stigler, Spence, and others on information theory. Nevertheless, the neoclassical method typically assumes no transaction or information costs unless some are specifically mentioned in the analysis.

8. Israel M. Kirzner, *Competition and Entrepreneurship* (Chicago: University of Chicago Press, 1973).

9. Both Mises, in *Human Action* and Rothbard, in *Man, Economy, and State*, discuss an evenly rotating economy that corresponds to the neoclassical concept of equilibrium, but the Austrian emphasis is more on the process by which the economy tends toward equilibrium.

10. Mises, *Human Action*, pp. 255–56, notes that in an economy in equilibrium there is no role for entrepreneurs. The concept of entrepreneurship Mises considers is Knight's concept, not Coase's, to draw from the discussion of Chapter 8.

11. Armen A. Alchian, "Uncertainty, Evolution, and Economic Theory," *Journal of Political Economy* 58 (1950), pp. 211–21, makes the argument

that the forces of competition will eliminate firms that do not act like profit maximizers, so that firms will act like profit maximizers regardless of their intentions. This justifies profit maximization as a heuristic assumption.

12. Harvey Averch and Leland L. Johnson, "Behavior of the Firm under Regulatory Constraint," *American Economic Review* 52, no. 5 (December 1962), pp. 1052–69.

13. This observation follows the theme of Donald M. McCloskey, "The Rhetoric of Economics," *Journal of Economic Literature* 21, no. 7 (June 1983), pp. 481–517.

14. See Robert Nozick, *Philosophical Explanations* (Cambridge, Mass.: Belknap, 1981), p. 2, for a discussion of methodology along these lines.

15. James M. Buchanan, "What Should Economists Do?" *Southern Economic Journal* 30, no. 3 (January 1964), pp. 213–22. This article also appeared as the title essay in his book, *What Should Economists Do?* (Indianapolis: Liberty Press, 1979).

Chapter 10

EMPIRICAL MODELS IN ECONOMICS

But this bias does not mean that I refuse to follow philosophical reason where it leads. . . I do not stop philosophical reasoning until it leads me where I want to go; then I stop.

Robert Nozick (1981, p. 2).

The preceding chapter found an important distinction between the Austrian and neoclassical views of the world to be in how they viewed the relationship between their models and the facts of the real world. The Austrians are more interested in explanation while the neoclassicals are more interested in prediction. There is a significant difference; the model that explains everything predicts nothing. The more predictive content a model has, the fewer phenomena it is capable of explaining, because the more precise the prediction, the more real-world phenomena that are ruled out as outcomes within the model.

Empirical issues have been discussed earlier in the book as well. Chapter 3 contained the argument that economics is fundamentally an empirical science, meaning that the fundamental economic axioms must come from empirical observation. More directly, Chapter 5 on positivism considered the idea that models can be evaluated based on their ability to predict. Previous chapters have argued the importance of empirical observation in economics. The purpose of this chapter is to look into the role of empirical models in economics in more detail.

McCloskey has made the observation that economists do not always do what they say they do,[1] and this is probably at least as true in empirical work in economics as in any other area. The quotation by Nozick at the beginning of the chapter suggests one problem of method that exists in econometrics and in any other type of reasoning. A researcher may have a preconceived notion about the correct answer, so rejects findings not in accord with the answer and continues to search, until at last "truth" is found. The numbers, which may appear to be objective evidence to the researcher and subsequent readers of the research, are not as objective as they first appear.

The 1980s have seen some serious work by econometricians comparing the results of actual empirical work with what is described, and this chapter will look into that literature later on. The chapter will begin by looking into the fundamental purposes of empirical models in economics.

PREDICTING AND OBSERVING IN ECONOMICS

All empirical models are not used for the same purpose. One reason why one might employ an empirical model in economics is to try to forecast what will happen in the future. The usefulness of economic forecasts (if they are accurate) is so obvious that the use of economic models to predict the future does not need to be justified. There are innumerable reasons why one might desire to foresee future events, and empirical models can be of help, but again, only if they are accurate.

It might at first appear that forecasts can be made without empirical models. For example, with knowledge of microeconomic theory, one could have forecast that the formation of the OPEC oil cartel in the early 1970s would have led to higher oil prices, and that because cartels are inherently unstable, eventually the cartel would break down and prices would decline after it deteriorated. No empirical model is necessary, and in fact the econometric forecasts about this very event did not appear after the fact to be any more accurate than predictions that could have been made simply by gathering facts from the newspaper.

A bit more thought about this example reveals that a forecast cannot be made without an empirical model, however. The theory of cartels does not tell one whether a cartel has formed or whether the price in the relevant market has risen. This can only be discovered by observing the real world. Thus, even the armchair theorist is using an empirical model, armed with real-world data, although without any sophisticated econometric technique. Theories cannot be applied to the real world without real-world data, and the combination of a theory with the relevant data makes an empirical model.[2] Prediction in economics cannot be a matter of theory alone. Any prediction requires an empirical model of some sort.

The armchair theorist in the above example was able to use data from simple observation of the real world as an empirical foundation for making a prediction, and often this technique can yield significant insights into the real world with limited effort. Economic theory combined with only a small amount of data can be a powerful tool for understanding the real world. Data can be obtained by looking out the window or reading the newspaper, and meaningful empirical statements can be made with this type of data alone. If a city enacts rent controls, a shortage of rental housing will result. Just an announcement of rent controls can therefore provide enough data to make a prediction with important policy implications.

Predictions of this sort are relatively easy to make because there is a relatively small data set involved. For more complex questions, the data are not very easy to understand unless they are organized in a meaningful way. How does monetary policy affect real output? As in the above problem, there are some theoretical answers available without resorting to statistics or econometrics, but even with a problem involving aggregated data like this, a more precise answer to the problem can be formulated by organizing the data using econometric modeling techniques. This will be even more true if the question being pursued deals with a multitude of firms or individuals.

Seen in this way, an econometric model is just another way of looking at the data in the real world. It is more sophisticated than looking out the window, but the underlying principle is the same. It is a way of finding out what has happened in some real-world event. Tests of statistical significance are obviously useful for determining whether what was observed was a matter of chance or is really a systematic change. One observes, for example, that in states that aggressively enforce the death penalty, murder rates are usually lower. Is this a coincidence, or are people responding to the increased cost of committing murder?

An econometric model can organize the data to see if the relationship that appears (with a look out the window) to be there is really there when a large number of cases are examined, and can also assess the statistical significance of the relationship to provide an idea of how likely it is that the observed phenomena could have arisen by chance.[3]

Econometric models, then, are tools for organizing observations about the real world. The world is complex, and some relationships within it can be more clearly grasped within the framework of an econometric model, just as others can be more clearly grasped with a microscope or X-ray machine. In addition, if the model accurately represents real-world relationships, it can be used to predict. The chapter on positivism presented the argument that accurate assumptions enhance the probability that a model that accurately depicts historical data will also accurately represent future movements in the same data, so that idea need only be mentioned here. In summary, empirical models are tools for observing the real world and predicting future occurrences.

Econometric models are also often used to test theoretical models. Some issues relating to empirical tests have been discussed before. The next section considers the possibility of empirical tests of economic models.

EMPIRICAL TESTS

An empirical test of a theory examines data described in a model which embodies the theory to see whether the data of the real world is consistent with the prediction of the theory. As the positivist argument goes, an empirical test cannot prove a theory to be true, since other possible theories might also be consistent with the same data, but empirical evidence inconsistent with the theory could falsify the theory. As noted several times previously, this positivist notion of empirical testing has fallen out of favor. A theory is surrounded by a protective belt of assumptions, and in reality, if the data do not agree with the theory, the theory is rarely discarded. Rather, the theorist argues that one or more of the assumptions have not been met.[4]

Following this line of reasoning, models cannot actually be tested empirically, although it is possible to find data consistent with a theory. An empirical test, then, is an examination of data to see if the data is consistent with the model being tested. The theory can never be tested because of the protective belt of assumptions that are necessary to map the ideas of the theory into the data of the real world, but the model—including all of the assumptions embedded in the data—can be tested to see if it is consistent.

ECONOMETRIC METHOD IN THEORY AND IN FACT

Econometric models rest on a foundation of statistical assumptions. Error terms are normally distributed, there is no heteroskedasticity, time series data are not serially correlated, and so forth. These assumptions may be hard to meet, but if they are not met, the statistical significance of the results is in question. Another important assumption that is made is that the data being examined is a random sample from the population on which inferences are being made. This section will examine this assumption critically in light of the possibilities opened up as a result of the computer.

Consider a simple statistics problem. An urn contains 1000 colored balls, some red and some white. An individual draws a sample of 100 balls and finds 10 red and 90 white balls in the sample. After drawing the balls, the individual might also draw the conclusion that the probability of drawing a red ball on the next draw is 10 percent. This assumes a random sample, however, and another possibility is that there are the same number of red balls as white balls, but the red balls were put in the urn first so the white balls are mostly on top. If the individual draws from the top of the urn, the probability of drawing a red ball will continually increase the larger the sample drawn.

The validity of econometric models rests on the same assumption of a random sample, but the assumption is violated more and more frequently with the use of the computer in econometric modelling. Before the advent of the computer, the computations involved in running a linear regression model made linear regression a time-intensive task. One would carefully specify the model, then collect the data and compute (by hand) the regression coefficients. Again, the results assumed a random sample to make inferences about the population, and the assumption was more likely to be satisfied then than today, when many specifications of the model can be run and compared with one another.

As a corollary to this idea, this paragraph begins a slight digression on the meaning of significance levels when estimating regressions on aggregate data, such as GNP, the price level, aggregate investment, and so forth. A significance level tells the researcher how confident one can be that the variables in the population are correlated with one another, given the relationship estimated in the regression model which comes from a sample of the population in which one is interested. As such, significance levels would seem to be meaningless when aggregate data is being used. For example, if one were to estimate a regression equation which used the money stock as an independent variable to explain nominal income, the resulting coefficient would be the relationship between the two variables. Since the model used all of the data—the population, and not a sample from the population—the researcher can be 100 percent confident that the coefficients in the model show the true relationship between the variables. If the coefficient is not zero, then it is not zero, and that is that.

This contrasts with the case where a sample is being used, and from the regression results in the sample, one uses a test of statistical significance to find the probability that the relationship in the regression could have been found from the sample when in fact the variables in the population are not related. Such a test would be meaningless, however, if the entire population is contained in the data set. What meaning could a significance level have under these conditions?

There are answers to this question, although the answers stretch the strict interpretation of significance levels as applying to samples of a population. One answer is that the real world we live in is but one of an infinite number of possible alternative worlds, so even aggregate data is only a sample of all of the possible data sets that could exist. Another similar answer is that the investigator is interested in the robustness of the results, for example, to use in forecasting future events. Thus, historical data is a subset of all possible data, which includes events that have not yet occurred. This interesting issue of the meaning of statistical significance when aggregate data is being used will not be pursued here, but the reader is welcome to consider it further.

The issue at hand is the assumption of a random sample in econometric models, which at one time might have been valid when regressions were calculated by hand, but would seem not to apply in the computer era. The reason is that many regressions can be run examining the same relationship, at very low cost. Subsets of the sample can be used. Variables can be added or deleted. Variables can be run in logs. In short, there are a host of creative techniques that can be used to search for a good statistical relationship in the data. The problem is that tests of statistical significance assume that the data being used is a random sample, and if it has been searched through to produce the particular numbers used in the test, then it is not a random sample. Such a search would be time-consuming before the use of the computer in econometrics, but since the advent of the computer, searches like this are done routinely.

SPECIFICATION SEARCH AND DATA MINING

Searching through data to get a good statistical fit goes by a number of names, including specification search and data mining. When a specification search is undertaken, the researcher looks at alternative specifications of a model in order to find the one that best fits the data. The resulting model is the most accurate representation of the true relationships in the real world, at least among the specifications searched. With data mining, the researcher goes through a data set looking for statistically significant relationships in order to support a hypothesis (or, perhaps, just in search of a publishable result). The greater the level of statistical significance, the more credible will be the result, so the researcher mines the data to find the relationship that is most significant. Specification search sounds like a noble research activity designed to model the real world as accurately as possible while data mining sounds like fishing around for the best statistical results, but the actual activities undertaken in both cases are just about the same.[5]

There may be an ethical distinction between the person searching for the best specification of a model and a person looking through a mass of data trying to find a publishable result, but tests of statistical significance do not make ethical distinctions. In both cases, the data ultimately used in the model are not a random sample, so in both cases traditional tests of statistical significance will overstate the true significance of the results. For example, with random data one would expect about one out of 20 coefficients to be significant at the .05 level. Thus, by searching through 100 random independent variables, one would expect to find five that are significant at the .05 level, which could then be combined into a regression equation that would contain only statistically significant variables, using a level of significance commonly used in economics.

Specification Search and Statistical Significance

In the example just given, if only the single equation with the five significant variables is reported as a research result, the result would appear to be very significant (in a statistical sense), whereas an evaluation of the entire search that generated the result shows that the result would have been expected if the numbers used to begin with were random. Clearly, one must take account not only of the reported statistical results but also the search process that was used to generate them in order to attach a meaningful level of statistical significance to them. Specification search increases the probability of finding results that are "statistically significant" using traditional statistical tests.

As a simple illustration of this, my colleague Steven Caudill and I tested the hypothesis that $Y = f(X1)$, all other things held equal, using random numbers for data. Our specification search was simple. We generated six other possible independent variables $X2 \ldots X7$, also random numbers, and generated 60 observations for each variable. The specification search was undertaken by looking at all possible combinations of X2 . . . X7 as independent variables along with X1 which was the subject of the hypothesis to be tested, and the data set was divided in half and the same search run on only half of the data. Only one half was used in this way, although both could have been. Our goal was to find a significant relationship between Y and X1.

This specification search was undertaken 100 times. That is, after searching the random data set for a significant relationship, another set of random numbers was generated and the search was run again, and so forth for 100 iterations. The specification search was quite limited, but out of the 100 data sets, results significant at the .05 level, as indicated by a t-test, were generated in 17 of the sets. In other words, using random numbers, this simple specification search was able to find results "significant at the 5 percent level" 17 percent of the time.

The specification search undertaken here is typical in economics. For example, the selecting of independent variables from among X2 . . . X7 would occur when one decides to leave out a variable from the equation, to use M1 instead of M2 for the money supply, or to use the corporate AAA bond rate rather than the 90-day Treasury Bill rate for an interest rate. While we did not do so in this simple example, a specification search might have also included searching for a better fitting dependent variable. It is common practice to add or delete variables from a regression equation as in this example, and in the real world, many more than six other variables might be searched through in this way.

The second part of the search involved deleting half of the sample. It is also common to delete part of a sample. Often, for example, the war years will be excluded. It is possible to use data from 1950 to the present or from 1900 to the present. Drawing data from different samples and selecting the best fit obviously violates the assumption of a random sample, but it is not uncommon to see researchers admitting to deleting part of their samples, and some unreported altering of a sample probably also occurs.

With only these two tools of data mining, the probability of getting a significant result went from 5 percent to 17 percent in our search. Other possibilities would have been to search for

new Y and X1 variables, as already suggested, to use log trans-
formations on some of the variables, to take first differences, to
divide through by one of the variables (e.g., take all variables
as a percent of GNP or something similar), or a host of other
data manipulations. With all of these possibilities, the researcher determined to get a statistically significant result can probably
find one.

Specification Search and Coefficient Bias

Not only will levels of reported statistical significance be affected by specification searches, coefficients will be biased from the
process as well. The logic behind the coefficient bias is relatively
straightforward.[6] Assume that one's theory is that X causes Y. In
this case, a regression equation with Y as the dependent variable
and X as one of the independent variables can be used to estimate the relationship between X and Y. The higher the t-value
associated with the coefficient on X, the better the specification
of the model, as argued in the above section. Since the t-value is
the coefficient on the variable (in this case, X) divided by the coefficient's variance, there are two things that could increase the
t-value for a given coefficient. The coefficient could be larger
in absolute value, or the variance could be smaller. This being
the case, a specification search for the best fitting specification
will tend to pick those with larger coefficients on the variables
in question because larger coefficients will tend to be associated with larger t-values on the variables.

The result is that when specification searches are undertaken
where the searcher considers high t-values to be an indication of
a good model specification, the absolute values of the coefficients
on the variables in the model will be biased upward. Thus, for
example, if the empirical results under consideration have been
subject to a specification search, estimates of demand elasticities
or multipliers will be biased away from zero as a result of the
search.

As bad as the whole matter seems, it is actually worse when
considered in the aggregate, and it is to that aggregate situation
that the next situation turns.

THE PUBLICATION FILTER

In economics, publishable statistical results tend to be statistically significant results. Since a major goal of research in economics is to publish the results, this provides the incentive for researchers to mine through their data for statistically significant results. But even if individual researchers do not do so, the publication policies of journals provide the same result as if the data were mined for the significant results.[7]

This will be true because a researcher will know that insignificant results will not be publishable and will not pursue them. One might imagine, then, 100 researchers with data sets of random numbers, and five of those find statistically significant results and send them off to journals. The journals publish the results, and even though the individual researchers did not engage in data mining themselves, the end result is the same. Frank Denton has referred to this as the publication filter.[8]

Following along with the arguments from the previous section, results that appear to be statistically significant when examined by themselves may be only random results reported from the 5 percent of researchers who happened to get statistically significant results. They may also be the results of a specification search by the author, but the point here is that even if they are not, the publication filter is an analog to the specification search process, ensuring that the results reported in journals are not drawn from a random sample. One can expect, therefore, that the true statistical significance of the reported results is lower than the significance level reported, and that the coefficients reported in empirical results are biased away from zero. The publication filter implies this even if no specification search is undertaken by any of the individual researchers.

The publication filter may actually be more subtle and more complex than what has been suggested above, because for understandable reasons, journal editors do not want to publish unreasonable results. This means that results must pass some test of reasonableness. Many qualifications of reasonableness will be apparent to economists. Demand curves slope downward, for example, so there will be an inverse relationship between the price of a good and the quantity demanded. A direct relationship will not be evidence of an upward sloping demand curve, but rather will be evidence of a misspecified demand equation. The researcher can then go about correcting the specification (with the implications discussed above). One might consider what types of results would appear in journals if there were no standards of reasonableness with which to filter the results ahead of time.

If one already knows what a reasonable answer is ahead of time, there would seem to be little reason for empirical work to find that reasonable answer. Empirical work would be most valuable when there is some question as to the correct answer. One question that falls into the unanswered category in the 1980s is whether taxpayers capitalize their future tax liabilities due to the future tax burden of the national debt. This would seem to provide an excellent case study for the way in which empirical work in economics can resolve these difficult empirical questions.

A Case Study

The contemporary story on this question begins with the publication of an article by Robert Barro in 1974.[9] Barro argued that there would be no real (as opposed to nominal) difference between financing a given level of government expenditures through borrowing as opposed to taxation. His argument in brief was that the present value of the future tax liabilities due to government borrowing would be exactly equal to the amount of taxation that would be needed to finance the expenditure without borrowing. Therefore, rational taxpayers will save to offset any government borrowing, leaving the same amount of consumption, saving, and investment that would have taken place with taxation. Barro's argument went against the popular view that government borrowing would crowd out private investment.

In its simplest form, the argument can be illustrated by an example. Assume that the government is going to spend $100, financed through taxation. This will have certain real effects. Now assume that, all else constant, the government decides to reduce taxes by $100 and increase its borrowing by $100. This provides taxpayers with $100 in additional disposable income. The additional consumption caused by this $100 increase in disposable income is what causes the crowding out effect, because with more income spent on consumption, less is available for private saving and investment. But Barro points out that the additional $100 asset is offset by a $100 liability due to the fact that in the future taxpayers will have to pay taxes to finance the government's present borrowing. The present value of these future taxes is just equal to the decline in present taxes, so the rational taxpayer will save an amount equal to the tax cut to finance the future tax payments.

If the interest rate were 10 percent, for example, the interest on the new $100 in government debt would be $10 per year, which would be financed by future taxes. The present value of this future liability would be $100, which just offsets the $100 tax reduction. The rational thing to do, then, is to take the $100 tax reduction money and put it in the bank, earning the interest rate of 10 percent. The proceeds can then be used to pay the taxes from the future interest on the debt. If the taxpayer does not do this, then the taxpayer is in effect allowing the government to force her to take out a loan which the taxpayer otherwise would not have wanted. Stated differently, if any of the $100 tax cut is used for consumption, the government's borrowing has forced the taxpayer to alter her pattern of intertemporal consumption, but by saving the $100 the taxpayer's intertemporal consumption pattern would remain the same regardless of whether taxation or debt is used to finance the government's expenditures. A simple application of the utility maximizing axiom leads to the conclusion that there will be no real differences between taxation and debt in public finance.

For present purposes Barro's specific argument is not as important as the fact that some very reputable economists disagreed strongly with his conclusions.[10] Thus, unlike the demand curve, which everyone knows slopes downward, there is disagreement among economists about whether taxation and debt are equivalent in their real effects. This would seem to provide a good opportunity for some empirical work to clarify an issue on which there is disagreement in theory about what happens in the real world.

As this chapter is being written, there has been over a decade of empirical work done on the subject, but while (perhaps) economists have made some progress on understanding the underlying issues, the profession is no closer to agreement on the fundamental question about whether taxation and debt are equivalent in their real effects. For example, in 1985 Reid found that taxation and debt were not equivalent in their real effects, while in the same year Evans found that they were.[11] In 1982 Feldstein published evidence refuting Barro's hypothesis, while in the next year Kormendi published empirical evidence supporting Barro.[12] In a 1974 study—published the same year as Barro's controversial article—Kochin found that taxpayers only partially account for future tax liabilities.[13] This conclusion was supported by Seater and by Holcombe, Jackson, and Zardkoohi, but in two separate studies, Tanner found that taxpayers fully discount their future tax liabilities.[14]

A simple examination of the record shows that at least in this case when there is theoretical disagreement on a particular issue regarding the real world, more than a decade of empirical work on the subject is not able to narrow the disagreement. As discussed at the beginning of the chapter, econometric techniques are simply tools for organizing facts when looking at the real world. But in this case the empirical examination of the real world has not been able to point to a single answer when in theory the answer to the question is unresolved. The answer may be ambiguous in theory, but when looking at the same real world, only one answer can be true in fact.

The Protective Belt

In trying to draw some general lessons from this particular case, one can see how the protective belt of assumptions that surround a theory can prevent the theory from being tested in the way that positivism would imply. One cannot directly look at taxpayers and see how they would act under some hypothetical different circumstances as compared to how they actually act in the real world, so some assumptions are required. If future tax liabilities are not fully discounted, then consumers should consume more and save less if more debt financing is used. Since the same taxpayers cannot be placed in different hypothetical worlds, some assumptions are required right away to hold all other things equal in a time series or cross-sectional analysis. One could examine changes in consumption or changes in saving. One could also look at changes in private investment caused by changes in saving, or since investment is inversely related to the interest rate, one could examine how deficit financing affects interest rates to test Barro's proposition. Then there are questions about model specification to accurately hold all other things equal.

One would hope that however the researcher went about looking at the problem, the answer would be the same. However, the case of the national debt controversy discussed above indicates that at least in some instances a decade of empirical research will not resolve theoretical ambiguities. In light of these empirical ambiguities that can arise, and in light of the statistical ambiguities that present themselves when computer intensive specification searches are undertaken, it is reasonable to take a look into the methodology of empirical economics to see if some methodological improvements suggest themselves.

EMPIRICAL EVIDENCE

The statistical tests that economists use in empirical work in general assume that the statistics being tested for significance are the only ones being looked at by the researcher. For example, using the t-values of the coefficients in a regression equation as a test of the statistical significance of the coefficient, the t-table assumes that the data points are a random sample of the population data. As already noted, this assumption will be violated if alternate specifications of a model are examined. Unfortunately, there are no easily available ways of testing significance levels when many different specifications of a problem have been examined. Stated simply, the tests of statistical significance commonly used are not appropriate for the methods actually used by economists using computers to generate their results.

It is not uncommon for economists to report their results as if the reported specification of the problem was the only one examined, and it is also not uncommon for economists to report that other specifications were examined, but then to use standard tests of significance on the specification(s) reported. In light of the earlier discussion of this chapter, the reported significance levels will not be a true reflection of the statistical significance of the results.

This section was titled empirical evidence to lead up to the question, evidence of what? When empirical results are presented in a paper, the reader has every reason to be skeptical, thinking that one out of twenty random coefficients will be significant at the .05 level. Has the researcher done something with the data, such as examine 100 coefficients and report only the five that were (randomly) significant at the .05 level? Perhaps this researcher did not do so, but the publication filter excluded from consideration nineteen other studies with insignificant results.

The remainder of this section makes some modest suggestions for ways that the reader of econometric research might be given more information about the empirical question under consideration. This goal has two aspects to it. First, the reader should be in a better position to judge the significance of the empirical results, and second, the empirical work should be done in such a way as to generate as much information as possible from the data. The specific suggestions that follow are along the lines of those proposed by numerous writers on econometric methodology. While statisticians have been aware of these types of problems for quite a while, recognition of them in economics journals has only begun in the 1980s.[15]

Report What Was Done

According to some ideal notion of how statistical tests in regression models are done, a theory is developed which specifies the model to be tested. Then the researcher gathers the data specified in the model, and then runs the regression. The results of this one test are then reported, along with statistics to indicate the level of statistical significance. If this is what actually was done, then the results should be reported this way, but in reality, more empirical work than this often is done, and often it is not reported. Sometimes an allusion to other independent variables is made in a footnote, or sometimes it is mentioned that some or all of the variables were tried as logs or first differences. In order to provide complete information to the reader, the reporting of empirical results should include at least a description of everything that was done, and ideally should report all of the results as well. Sometimes the reporting of all of the results would take an excessive amount of space if a large number of specifications were run, but at least the reader should be informed about what alternate specifications were tried and in general what the results were.

The point here is simply that in order for the reader to be able to judge the statistical significance of the results, everything that was tried to get those results must be reported. One would be skeptical of the results if, for example, it was reported that out of a thousand different specifications examined, only the one that appeared in the paper was "statistically significant."

Examine and Report Plausible Alternate Specifications

A specification search changes the meaning of significance tests, but this is not a reason for not doing one. In fact, a specification search will help to indicate how robust the results of an empirical test are. In the spirit of data mining, one might examine a multitude of specifications until the one supporting the researcher's hypothesis was discovered, and then just report that one. But the researcher might also, by accident, examine the one specification that supports the hypothesis first. The researcher could then honestly report that result along with the standard significance tests.

If this is all that is done, the researcher foregoes the opportunity to find out more from the data. With the computer as a tool, it is easy to examine many plausible alternate specifications of a model, and this should be done to give the reader (and the researcher) an indication of how robust the results of the model are. If such a specification search is not undertaken, the researcher is stopping short of finding out everything that could be discovered about the hypothesis being examined in the empirical work.

Consider, for example, an independent variable that is found to be significant at the .05 level in a regression, suggesting that that variable is correlated with the dependent variable. If ten different specifications of the model were examined and the independent variable was significant at the .05 level every time, this would be stronger evidence than if the independent variable were significant in, say, only two of the ten specifications tried. If all of these trials and results were reported, the reader would have much more information available for judging the strength of the statistical results than if only one specification were reported.

The two recommendations made here would go a long way toward increasing the value of published econometric results. In summary, the recommendations are, first, to examine many different plausible specifications of a model rather than looking at just one. This commonsense recommendation says nothing more than that one should try to find as much information in the data as is available. With the computer available as a tool, this should be expected in econometric research. The second recommendation is to report everything that has been done to generate the empirical results. The reader will have much more information on which to evaluate the results if the total process is reported. These are modest suggestions, to be sure, and have been made by others. Find out as much as possible from the data, and report everything that was done to generate the results.

EXPLORING DATA

The presentation of empirical work in economics is heavily influenced by positivism. Economists present a model and then report the results of a test. As already noted, the data are often probed much more than would be called for in a simple test, which makes test statistics less meaningful, but enhances understanding of the data if all of the probing that was done is reported. In fact, by searching for better specifications, by looking for better explanatory variables (M1 or M2? Corporate bond rate or federal funds rate?), economists are looking at the world to see how things relate to each other. For simple phenomena, a look out the window can reveal much, but with much complex data, the tools of statistics help reveal patterns that might go unnoticed without some type of summary measures.

Despite the rhetoric of economics that frames most statistics as statistical tests, the tools of statistics are most often used to summarize complex phenomena to identify relationships among variables. This is partly due to the problems with positivism already discussed at length and partly due to the fact that the actual methods that economists follow do not adhere to the rhetoric of positivism anyway. Statistical tools can help people see complex relationships in data in the same way that binoculars can help people see what is happening in the distance. The increasing sophistication of computer hardware and software allows economists to understand more about the relationships in the data they use.

Economists are becoming aware of the potential for misleading results due to data mining, but have not escaped from the methodological constraints of positivism. Statisticians, meanwhile, have been developing principles for exploratory data analysis, where the idea is not to test for statistically significant relationships but to analyze the data to see what relationships are there.[16] Regardless of how widespread the specific methods advocated by those statisticians pursuing exploratory data analysis become, econometrics could provide much more reliable empirical results if it explicitly recognized that much econometric work is a search of the data for relationships rather than statistical testing. Explicit recognition will have the benefits both of more honest and easily interpreted results and of orienting the frontiers of econometrics toward development of the tools most appropriate for exploring the data.

CONCLUSION

Economists are often suspicious of empirical work done by others in their profession, and often with justification. The standard way in which empirical results are reported frequently bears little similarity to the way in which the results were actually generated. One problem is that methodology in econometrics has not kept up with the technology of computer generated results.

Econometrics simply provides standard tools for looking at the data in the real world. Is an apparent pattern actually there? Could a relationship that seems to exist merely be the result of chance, or would it be unlikely that such a pattern could be generated randomly? Economists need some method for analyzing large amounts of data that can not readily be understood by simple observation. Econometrics provides the tools.

By searching through the data and selectively reporting results, a researcher can mislead others (and perhaps himself) about the true nature of the relationships in the data. Since journals are selective about what they publish and researchers are selective about what they send to journals, there is good reason to be suspicious about published econometric results.

The suspicions could be lessened if it became standard econometric practice to examine and report plausible alternate formulations of econometric models. Econometric results reported under the assumption that the data examined are from a random sample of the population data were appropriate in the pre-computer era when regression results calculated by hand were time-consuming so that the researcher could be justified in choosing the most plausible specification ahead of time and running just that specification. But today there is no reason not to take advantage of the capabilities of the computer to find out more about the data being analyzed.

Empirical work provides a method of examining the world, but too often published empirical work gives only a selective view. The problem with empirical work in economics does not derive from what the empirical work is, but rather from what it is not but claims to be. Empirical work often claims to be testing a theory, but discussion throughout the book has shown that it is not possible to test theories by themselves. The necessary assumptions provide a protective belt that prevents the possibility of an empirical test in that sense. Empirical work also often claims significant results based on reported results that are incomplete when measured against the standard of what results could be reported given the power of the computer. The problem may just be that econometric methodology has not kept up with advances in computer technology, but there is hope that the situation will change. Articles in generally read economics journals in the 1980s are making economists more aware of the problems discussed in this chapter. These methodological advances can pave the way toward making empirical work more informative about economic relationships in the real world.

NOTES

1. Donald M. McCloskey, "The Rhetoric of Economics," *Journal of Economic Literature* 21, no. 7 (June 1983), pp. 481–517.

2. It is not the only way to make an empirical model, however. An empirical model could simply be a search through data for statistical patterns, so no theory would be necessary. This is, for example, an important way that empirical models are built in medical research.

3. On this subject, see Isaac Ehrlich, "The Deterrent Effect of Capital Punishment: A Question of Life and Death," *American Economic Review* 65, no. 3 (June 1975), pp. 397–417.

4. This notion of a protective belt of assumptions was developed by Imre Lakatos. See, for example, his *The Methodology of Scientific Research Programmes*, vol. I (Cambridge: Cambridge University Press, 1978).

5. The term data mining was used by Michael C. Lovell, "Data Mining," *Review of Economics and Statistics* 65, no. 1 (February 1983), pp. 1–12.

6. The conclusions in this section are derived mathematically in Steven B. Caudill and Randall G. Holcombe, "Coefficient Bias Due to Specification Search in Econometric Models," *Atlantic Economic Journal* 15, no. 3 (September 1987), pp. 30–34.

7. For an early observation of this see Gordon Tullock, "Publication Decisions and Tests of Significance," *Journal of the American Statistical Association* 54 (September 1959), p. 593.

8. See Frank T. Denton, "Data Mining as an Industry," *Review of Economics and Statistics* 68, no. 1 (February 1985), pp. 124–27.

9. Robert J. Barro, "Are Government Bonds Net Wealth?" *Journal of Political Economy* 82 (November/December 1974), pp. 1095–1117.

10. See James M. Buchanan, "Barro on the Ricardian Equivalence Theorem," *Journal of Political Economy* 84 (April 1976), pp. 337–42, and Martin Feldstein, "Perceived Wealth in Bonds and Social Security: A Comment," *Journal of Political Economy* 84 (April 1976), pp. 331–36, for examples. Barro's "Reply to Feldstein and Buchanan," *Journal of Political Economy* 84 (April 1976), pp. 343–49, illustrates that Barro remained in disagreement with his critics.

11. Bradford G. Reid, "Aggregate Consumption and Deficit Financing: An Attempt to Separate the Permanent from Transitory Effects," *Economic Inquiry* 23, no. 3 (July 1985), pp. 475–86, and Paul Evans, "Do Large Deficits Produce High Interest Rates?" *American Economic Review* 75, no. 1 (March 1985), pp. 68–87.

12. Martin Feldstein, "Government Deficits and Aggregate Demand," *Journal of Monetary Economics* 9 (1982), pp. 1–20, and Roger C. Kormendi, "Government Debt, Government Spending, and Private Sector Behavior," *American Economic Review* 73, no. 5 (December 1983), pp. 994–1010.

13. Levis A. Kochin, "Are Future Taxes Anticipated by Consumers?" *Journal of Money, Credit, and Banking* 6, no. 3 (August 1974), pp. 385–94.

14. John J. Seater, "Are Future Taxes Discounted?" *Journal of Money, Credit, and Banking* 14 (August 1982), pp. 376–89; Randall Holcombe, John Jackson, and Asghar Zardkoohi, "The National Debt Controversy," *Kyklos* 34, Fasc. 2 (1981), pp. 186–202; J. Earnest Tanner, "An Empirical Investigation of Tax Discounting," *Journal of Money, Credit, and Banking* 11, no. 2 (May 1979), pp. 214–18; and Tanner, "Fiscal Policy and Consumer Behavior," *Review of Economics and Statistics* 61, no. 2 (May 1979), pp. 317–21.

15. See, for examples, Thomas Mayer, "Economics as a Hard Science: Realistic Goal or Wishful Thinking," *Economic Inquiry* 18, no. 2 (April 1980), pp. 165–78; Edward E. Leamer, "Let's Take the Con Out of Econometrics," *American Economic Review* 73, no. 1 (1983), pp. 31–43; and Donald N. McCloskey, "The Loss Function has been Mislaid: The Rhetoric of Significance Tests," *American Economic Review* 75, no. 2 (May 1985), pp. 201–205. Following up on Leamer's article, see also Michael McAleer, Adrian R. Pagan, and Paul A. Volker, "What Will Take the Con Out of Econometrics?" *American Economic Review* 75, no. 3 (June 1985), pp. 293–307, and Leamer's "Sensitivity Analysis Would Help," *American Economic Review* 75, no. 3 (June 1985), pp. 308–13.

16. An introduction to exploratory data analysis is found in John W. Tukey, *Exploratory Data Analysis* (Reading, Mass.: Addison-Wesley, 1977). See also Frederick Mosteller and John W. Tukey, *Data Analysis and Regression* (Reading, Mass.: Addison-Wesley, 1977); Paul F. Velleman and David C. Hoaglin, *Applications, Basics, and Computing of Exploratory Data Analysis* (Boston: Duxbury Press, 1981); and for a discussion of the rationale and development of the methods of exploratory data analysis, *Understanding Robust and Exploratory Data Analysis* (New York: John Wiley & Sons, 1983), and *Exploring Data Tables, Trends, and Shapes* (New York: John Wiley & Sons, 1985).

Chapter 11

ECONOMIC IMPERIALISM

> Our Hypothesis is trivial, for it merely asserts that we should apply standard economic logic as extensively as possible. But the self-same hypothesis is also a demanding challenge, for it urges us not to abandon opaque and complicated problems with the easy suggestion that the further explanation will perhaps someday be produced by one of our sister behavioral sciences.
>
> Gary S. Becker and George J. Stigler (1977, pp. 89–90).

If the breadth of a discipline were defined by its name, economics would be limited to an analysis of the production and distribution of wealth. By itself this would be a broad subject area, but economists have broadened their area of inquiry well beyond what is normally thought of as economics. The economic analysis of law is a thriving subdiscipline within economics that has its own specialists and its own journals. The subdiscipline of public choice uses economic analysis to study political institutions. Both of these areas are interdisciplinary, as lawyers contribute to the research in the economic analysis of law and political scientists participate in public choice. But economic analysis has branched out further than this, and has been used to explain biological phenomena as well as institutions such as marriage and child-bearing, and has dealt with aspects of human behavior as diverse as sports activities and criminal behavior. This chapter is devoted to an analysis of the overlap between economics and other disciplines. This often consists of using economic models to analyze phenomena generally thought to be noneconomic in nature, but sometimes also consists of the use of models from other disciplines to explain economic activity.

This type of inquiry seems appropriate in a discussion of economic methodology because it is really the methods and models of economics that have made it an enticing framework for analyzing phenomena that are not strictly considered economic. Chapter 6 on methodological individualism discussed this line of reasoning to a degree, and the present chapter will pick up where Chapter 6 left off. The chapter will then go on to an overview of some areas in which economics has interacted with other disciplines.

THE APPLICATION OF ECONOMIC MODELS

It is worth reconsidering at this point what defines the discipline of economics. Some areas of inquiry, such as physics, biology, and geology, are defined by their subject matter, but economics is far more than a study of the economy. In the social sciences, disciplines are less defined by their subject matter, although some, like psychology and political science, seem more circumscribed by a particular subject matter than others, such as sociology, anthropology, and economics. Even sociology and anthropology might be thought of as defined by a particular subject matter, although as their names indicate, the subject matter itself is broad.

The key for understanding how economics has extended well beyond the bounds of simply describing the operation of the economy lies in the simplicity of its underlying assumptions. Economics has the twin advantages that even the most complex economic models are based on only a few underlying assumptions, and that these few assumptions are accepted as axiomatic by an overwhelming majority of economists. Having agreed on a few simple tools, economists can then go about applying them to problems in the real world. Consider, for example, how much of economics could be understood simply by exploring the implications of utility maximization, diminishing marginal rates of substitution, opportunity cost, and the law of diminishing marginal returns.

Economic imperialists have gotten the most mileage from the application of the principles of utility maximization and diminishing marginal rates of substitution. Indeed, these concepts define the behavior of the stereotype economic man. Individuals will choose the option that they feel best furthers their own self-interest, and individuals will be more likely to choose an option if it becomes relatively cheaper. While these concepts seem relatively uncontroversial on the surface, they have aroused considerable controversy when applied to specific situations. Arguments against the economic notion of utility maximization seem to follow two lines. One is that individual behavior is much more complex than simply choosing what is in one's own self-interest, so that some choices will consciously be made that are against the individual's interest. The second is that with regard to some choices, individuals do not consider the costs involved when they make the choice.

There are two frequently used rebuttals to these arguments. The first is to make utility maximization a tautological concept, as in the Austrian theory discussed in Chapter 9. An individual must believe that the chosen option is the best one. Otherwise, the individual would have picked another option. The second frequently used rebuttal is empirical in nature. The implications of these assumptions about economic behavior provide a very accurate description of the real world. The accuracy of the conception of economic man need not be debated here, for it is the application of the concept that is of more interest to the notion of economic imperialism.

Chapter 6 presented the argument that the main contribution of economics to the world's knowledge was the development of laws of social behavior that were similar to the physical laws that had been known for centuries. Before the development of economics, scholars were unaware of laws defining regularities of social behavior. A great contribution of economics to social thought was the idea that social events could be analyzed within a predictable framework of causes and effects, just as was the case in the natural sciences. These laws of social behavior have had a powerful influence, but the reason why they have been able to expand beyond the confines of the original boundaries of economic science has as much to do with the simplicity of the fundamental principles as their comprehensive applicability.

The fundamental principles of economics are extremely easy to understand and apply, providing a good opportunity for them to be used on phenomena not ordinarily considered economic. For example, it is easy for an armchair theorist to speculate on how an entity might behave in order to best further its self–interest. The entity might be a politician, or might be a leaf on a tree trying to maximize the amount of sunlight that it receives. The entity might be an individual making a decision to get married, divorced, or have children, or could be an individual considering committing a crime. More sophisticated investigations are likely to follow from armchair theorizing that is so easy to begin, and formal economic analysis is ready to invade areas formerly considered beyond the domain of economics.

A book could be written on any one sub-area of economic imperialism, and indeed many have been. The remainder of this chapter will consider some of those areas, starting with the area of politics and law, which seems like the most natural area for economics to invade.

LAW AND POLITICS

Until the late 1800s, economics was combined with politics and studied as political economy. There were differences between the study of political institutions and the study of the economic effects of public policies, but while the study of politics and political economy were not quite the same, the appellation indicates the close link that scholars of the time saw between politics and economics. The link weakened during the first half of the 20th century for two reasons. First was the increased understanding of the technical aspects of economics which lead economists to study economic theory with a looser connection to economic reality. Second was the development of theories with implications that suggested active policy prescriptions. By 1950, the politics involved in political economy had disappeared and was replaced by a very sophisticated economic theory, at least if judged by the standards of a few decades earlier.[1]

The notion of more active policy implications is worth addressing because political economy has always brought with it policy recommendations. Before the 20th century, however, the policy implications typically were to leave the market to its own devices. This laissez faire type of recommendation requires relatively little understanding of politics to implement when compared to policy implications suggested by twentieth-century economics. Even the antitrust laws, which were instituted late in the 19th century, were not supported by the economists of the time.[2]

The 19th century did see the development of the theory of socialism, but the policy recommendation in this case was to replace one economic system with another. The replacement system was not thought out very well either, which led to the socialist calculation debate in the early part of the 20th century where the question was raised as to whether a socialist economy would be possible at all. Thus, some individuals were arguing for the market system to be replaced while others were arguing that government involvement in the economy should be reduced in order to allow the market economy to reach its full potential.

A middle ground became popular in the mid-20th century as a result of two developments in economic theory. The first was the popular acceptance of Keynesian economics and the notion of a managed capitalist economy. The second was the development of more sophisticated models of market equilibrium and optimal resource allocation which illustrated all of the problems that exist in theory to keep markets from allocating resources efficiently.[3] In both the Keynesian macroeconomics framework and the market failure framework, the policy implications ran along the lines of agreeing that the market system in an ideal setting could allocate resources optimally, but that in the imperfect real world, economists could provide policy makers with guidance to shape policies that would improve on the market's allocation of resources.

This line of reasoning embodied a double standard for human behavior. On the one hand, individuals in the market were behaving in their narrow self–interests, while on the other hand, policy makers were expected to follow the economist's good advice to improve the economy, with no regard paid to the incentives faced by the policy makers themselves. The subdiscipline of public choice, which emerged as a recognizable subdiscipline in economics in the last half of the 20th century, is founded on the

simple premise that people in the government can be expected
to act in their own self-interests just as is assumed about participants in the market.[4]

Matters of economic policy would seem to naturally suggest
themselves as candidates for this type of theory,[5] but economic
theory found itself considering strictly political matters, such as
voting and committee decisions, as well.[6] The economic analysis
of political decisions has not been without its critics, but it has
been widely enough accepted that public choice is a subdiscipline
in political science as well as in economics.

The interdisciplinary area of law and economics has seen the
same type of development. Economic theory has been a natural
part of the law in matters dealing with the economy, such as
antitrust law, but has found its domain expanding into other
areas as well. Richard Posner's important book on the economic
analysis of law[7] places the entire legal structure within an economic framework. Isaac Ehrlich's controversial article on capital
punishment argued that capital punishment provides enough of
a deterrent effect to murderers to prevent more murders than the
number of murderers executed for their crime.[8] From its origins
as the study of political economy, it would seem natural for economic theories to be applied to matters of politics and law, and
indeed they have.

The reason probably has less to do with the natural link in subject matter than the nature of economic models, however. There
was, after all, a narrowing of the subject matter at the end of the
19th century when political economy became economics. But the
development of economic theory into a set of tools with powerful
predictive ability based on a few easily understood premises is
what made it so natural to apply economics to the related areas of
politics and law. The tools of economics are easy enough to apply
and yield powerful enough predictions that they have expanded
well beyond these closely related areas.

OTHER AREAS OF APPLICATION

Isaac Ehrlich's article, just mentioned, provides an ideal example of the way in which economic models are applied to

phenomena not usually thought of as economic. As a simple application of the theory of utility maximization, Ehrlich reasoned that if the cost of committing murder rose, fewer people would choose to commit murder, just as if the cost of gasoline rose, fewer people would choose to buy gasoline. Ehrlich provided evidence to support his contention, but from the standpoint of the methodological issues raised, the conjecture itself is more interesting than the supporting evidence. Economic imperialism consists mostly of applying the simple premise that people will substitute out of something when the cost rises.

Much innovative work along these lines has been done by Gary Becker, who has seen that relative prices can influence decisions such as whether to marry, whom to marry, and how many children to have.[9] Once one sees the possibilities suggested by this type of analysis, it is easy to apply the model of economic man to any choices that individuals make. Indeed, why should one make market decisions such as how much steak to buy relative to hamburger any differently from decisions such as who to invite over to the cook-out, who to vote for in an election, and how much support to give to one's children? In all cases, it makes sense to assume that the individual will make the decision that will best further the decision maker's well-being.

The theory of economic behavior has been applied to animals as well as humans. In several studies, Battalio, Kagel, and others[10] have demonstrated that animals in experimental situations exhibit the same type of choice behavior that is described in neoclassical micro theory. In his famous treatise on methodology, Milton Friedman even suggested that the maximizing behavior described in economic theory could be applied to the behavior of plants.[11] These examples could be discussed in more detail,[12] but the point has been made that economic theory has gone well beyond explaining phenomena that are strictly considered economic.

Again, it is worth emphasizing that this economic imperialism has less to do with the subject matter being analyzed than with the way in which economics models phenomena. Economic models rest on a few solidly established axioms that are generally accepted by economists. This makes the basic economic model relatively easy to understand and relatively uncontroversial, at least in standard applications. Someone might question whether the particular model is appropriate for the task to which it is put, but the model itself is accepted as a good tool for something. Any controversy, therefore, is over how far the applications of the model can be stretched rather than over whether the model is useful at all.

In summary, economic models rest on fundamentally simple principles and are easily applied to a diverse range of subjects. This accounts for the success of the models in analyzing phenomena normally not considered economic. One would hope that a contributing factor would be that economic models have been successful in modeling general phenomena, but the models would not have been nearly so attractive if they had not been simple and generally accepted in their most obvious applications.

ECONOMICS AND BIOLOGY

Another discipline that might be called imperialistic is biology, not so much because biologists themselves are invading the turf of other scientists, but because biological models have been useful in understanding nonbiological phenomena. The theory of evolution in biology has the same characteristics of applicability that were credited to economic models in the previous section. The theory of evolution is generally accepted, it is simple and easy to understand, and therefore, it is easy to extend its applications to nonbiological phenomena.

In economics, the application of biological models has taken two forms. First, the notion of the survival of the fittest has been applied to economic entities in the same way that it has been applied to biological species.[13] Following along with this line of reasoning, firms that have the characteristics that allow them to survive will grow and prosper while those that do not will wither and die. Since profit maximization is the characteristic that firms must have to prosper, it stands to reason that the firms that engage in profit maximizing behavior will be the survivors.

The interesting thing about this line of reasoning is that firms do not have to be trying to maximize their profits. The ones that do will survive while the ones that do not will die. Meanwhile, imitators will imitate successful firms, the successful firms themselves will be able to grow because of their profits, implying that one does not have to identify profit maximizing behavior ahead of time or be able to know it when one sees it. Profit maximizing behavior will evolve in the economic system even if it is not a part of anyone's intention.

The notion of social Darwinism predates Darwin by at least a century, and scholars such as David Hume recognized that productive social institutions would flourish while counterproductive institutions would die. This type of reasoning applied to economics has been relatively uncontroversial, and indeed appears to be just another way—albeit a fruitful way—to state the same conclusions contained in Adam Smith's conjecture about the invisible hand.

The second way in which biological models have found their way into economics, and into social science in general, is through the theory of sociobiology. But whereas the notion of evolution in an economy is accepted generally as a good analogy for the way in which an economy operates, sociobiological notions have not been so universally accepted by economists.

SOCIOBIOLOGY

Edward Wilson has identified the central theoretical question in sociobiology as how altruism, "which by definition reduces personal fitness,"[14] can evolve through the process of natural selection. This question has natural interest to an economist because one of the central tenets of economic behavior is that individuals act in their own self-interests. Altruistic behavior would seem to be out of the question for a utility maximizing economic man.

There are several ways in which the utility maximizing model might be reconciled with altruistic behavior. The most straightforward is to make the argument that behavior which appears altruistic is really in the narrow self-interest of the individual, once the individual's complete environment is understood. For example, an individual who does something "unselfish" for

Figure 11.1
Prisoner's Dilemma Payoff Matrix

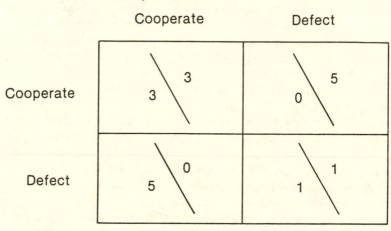

someone else builds good will so that at a later date someone else is more likely to behave unselfishly toward that individual.

A model of this type was developed by Robert Axelrod in his book, *The Evolution of Cooperation*.[15] Axelrod's conclusions are based upon the results of an iterative prisoners' dilemma game played by computer programs submitted by a number of individuals. Axelrod invited individuals to submit programs to play a prisoners' dilemma game in which the program could decide to cooperate or not cooperate with other programs that it played with. The lowest payoff resulted from cooperating with another program that did not cooperate, and the highest payoff resulted from not cooperating with another program that did cooperate. Two programs not cooperating with each other would receive a lower score than two programs that cooperated, however. The exact payoff matrix used in Axelrod's game is given in Figure 11.1.

As the prisoners' dilemma game is typically discussed, the game is only played once, and it is apparent from the payoff matrix that if one player cooperates, the best strategy for the other player is to not cooperate. Likewise, if the other player does not cooperate, the best strategy is still not to cooperate. However, when both players follow their own self-interests and do not cooperate, they end up getting a lower payoff than if they each had cooperated.

In Axelrod's game, players play against each other a large number of times (the number is not specified at the beginning of the game), and players can remember the outcomes of previous plays against other opponents. A large number of strategies were used, but the winning strategy in the several times that Axelrod ran the tournament, and with some variation in the play, was the simplest strategy submitted. This strategy, called "tit for tat," simply cooperated with another opponent the first time they met, and then did whatever the opponent did the previous time on their subsequent meetings. Therefore, if the other strategy always cooperated, tit for tat always cooperated. If the other strategy never cooperated, tit for tat cooperated only the first time and then did not cooperate from then on. If the other strategy started cooperating at any time, tit for tat would take that as an encouraging sign and would cooperate as long as the other strategy continued its cooperation.

The game was played against many other players and the winning strategy was the one with the most points against all opponents. Tit for tat was the consistent winning strategy, but it is interesting to note that tit for tat can never get more points interacting with an opponent than the opponent gets. Two co-operating strategies always get the same points, and since tit for tat starts by cooperating, it may get fewer points than an opponent. But although it cannot get more points cooperating with another strategy than the other strategy gets from its interactions with tit for tat, tit for tat outscores other opponents because that is the strategy that encourages other strategies to cooperate with it for high combined points.

Tit for tat sends the message that it will cooperate as long as you will, but if you do not cooperate, it will strike back by not cooperating, but will be willing to cooperate again if you want to. Axelrod goes into more detail about the game and strategies employed, but from this discussion it is apparent that, in Axelrod's game anyway, the strategy that maximizes the individual's self-interest is a cooperative strategy where individuals try to work together for their mutual benefit rather than try to take advantage of others and further their own narrow self-interest.

For present purposes, the significance of this finding is that behavior which outwardly appears altruistic may simply be behavior which is designed (consciously or unconsciously) to elicit the cooperation of others. As such, it furthers the narrow self interest of the individual and would be considered an example of the selfish utility maximizing behavior that is normally depicted in utility maximizing models in economics.[16]

A second method of reconciling altruistic behavior in a utility maximizing framework is to postulate that individuals have interdependent utility functions. One individual has as an argument in his utility function the well-being of another individual. In this case, the first person's altruistic behavior toward the second person indirectly increases the first person's utility by increasing the second person's utility. This motivation for altruistic behavior plays an important part in some economic models dealing with significant questions.[17]

The type of altruism modeled with interdependent utility functions runs directly into the question raised by Wilson about the survival of such traits. If there are altruistic and egoistic people, the altruists give up some of their well-being for others while the egoists do not, giving the egoists more resources to use in surviving and proliferating in their environment. Eventually, one would expect the altruistic trait to die out and for the egoistic trait to prosper. In a model of natural selection, then, how can altruism be selected as a surviving trait?

One answer is that, as discussed above, altruism helps one survive. For example, if one person gives to another, that provides the second person with an incentive to protect the well-being of the altruist, which will help the altruist to survive. Note that the recipient has an incentive to help the altruist even if the recipient has no altruistic qualities at all.[18] This again explains how altruistic behavior can be in the self-interest of the altruist even though on the surface the behavior appears to be selfless.

Another more controversial answer to the question of altruism looks critically at what is being selected through natural selection. It is not the individual, who will surely die, but the individual's genetic traits that will be genetically passed on from generation to generation. In this case, genetic traits are more likely to survive when the individuals who have those traits enhance not only their own survival chances, but also the chances of survival for those who carry the same traits. Therefore, altruistic behavior that is often observed among family members, while it may reduce the ability of the particular altruistic individual to survive, maximizes the probability that the individual's genetic traits will survive through the individual's relatives that carry the same (or similar) traits. Following this line of reasoning, one should be the most altruistic to one's immediate family, and should be more altruistic toward members of one's own race than those of other races. Could racism be a trait inherited and enhanced through natural selection?

One can immediately see why models that depict maximizing behavior at the genetic level rather than at the individual level could be controversial. But clearly some behavior is instinctive, and following maximizing principles, it would follow that those traits that best insured the survival of the gene pool would themselves survive, leading to the conclusion that behavior characteristics are at least partly determined by natural selection. The area of interaction between economics and biology is relatively uncharted, but raises some interesting questions.[19]

CONCLUSION

This chapter has provided only a brief excursion into the interaction of economics with other disciplines. While economics does borrow some from other disciplines—biology is an important example—much of the interaction comes from the application of economic models to phenomena normally considered outside the domain of economics. Economic imperialism is one appellation that has been given to this ever increasing domain of the application of economic principles.

The particular applications are of interest in their own right, but taken together they have interest from a methodological standpoint as well. It is worthwhile considering why economics has been relatively successful at invading the domain of other disciplines. One should not be surprised to find a good explanation in the way in which economists analyze questions.

At the foundation of economic analysis is a simple model of human behavior that is widely accepted by economists. While the model is simple—or more likely because the model is simple—it has a great deal of predictive ability. This allows economic models to readily draw out implications in any instance where human behavior is involved. In fact, examples in this chapter have shown that economic implications can be discovered in cases of animal and plant behavior as well. The economic axiom of utility maximizing behavior goes a long way toward explaining so much of what can be observed in the world that economists, while they may tend to overapply their models of the world, are prone to constantly observe examples of economic behavior in their everyday lives. In an interesting extrapolation of this phenomenon, several mystery novels have been written in which the clues require the application of economic principles to decipher.[20]

One of the reasons that economic imperialism is interesting is that it is a result of the methodology of economics. Economic methodology is based on the use of models that have a high degree of commonality regardless of the application or school of thought within economics. The models are simple, yet offer great predictive ability, lending themselves to diverse applications.

NOTES

1. An interesting discussion of the method of early economists is provided by William J. Baumol, "On Method in U. S. Economics a Century Earlier," *American Economic Review* 75, no. 6 (December 1985), pp. 1–12.

2. F.M. Sherer, *Industrial Market Structure and Economic Performance* (Chicago: Rand McNally & Co., 1970), p. 424, notes that economists at the time of the passage of the antitrust laws were unconcerned about the trusts, and viewed them as a natural response to economies of scale that were present due to industrial growth. The antitrust laws were actually enacted in response to the demands of special interests. See Bruce Benson, M. L. Greenhut, and Randall G. Holcombe, "Interest Groups and the Antitrust Paradox," *Cato Journal* 6, no. 3 (Winter 1987), pp. 801–17.

3. Francis M. Bator, "The Anatomy of Market Failure," *Quarterly Journal of Economics* 72 (August 1958), pp. 351–79, is a classic article in this tradition.

4. See James M. Buchanan, "Public Finance and Public Choice," *National Tax Journal* 28 (December 1975), pp. 383–94, for a discussion along these lines.

5. An example is George J. Stigler's "The Theory of Economic Regulation," *Bell Journal of Economics and Management Science* 2 (Spring 1971), pp. 3–21.

6. Two of the important early works in the area are Anthony Downs, *An Economic Theory of Democracy* (New York: Harper and Row, 1957), and James M. Buchanan and Gordon Tullock, *The Calculus of Consent* (Ann Arbor: University of Michigan Press, 1962).

7. Richard A. Posner, *Economic Analysis of Law* (Boston: Little, Brown, 1972).

8. Isaac Ehrlich, "The Deterrent Effect of Capital Punishment: A Question of Life and Death," *American Economic Review* 65, no. 3 (June 1975), pp. 397–417.

9. For examples of some of Becker's work, see Gary S. Becker, *The Economic Approach to Human Behavior* (Chicago: University of Chicago Press, 1976), and *Treatise on the Family* (Cambridge: Harvard University Press, 1981).

10. See, for examples, Raymond C. Battalio, Leonard Green, and John H. Kagel, "Income-Leisure Tradeoffs of Animal Workers," *American Economic Review* 71, no. 4 (September 1981), pp. 621–32; Raymond C. Battalio, John H. Kagel, Howard Rachlin, and Leonard Green, "Commodity-Choice Behavior with Pigeons as Subjects," *Journal of Political Economy* 89, no. 1 (February 1981), pp. 67–91; and John H. Kagel, Raymond C. Battalio, Howard Rachlin, Leonard Green, Robert L. Basmann, and W. R. Klem, "Experimental Studies of Consumer Demand Using Laboratory Animals," *Economic Inquiry* 13 (March 1975), pp. 22–38.

11. See the opening essay in Milton Friedman, *Essays in Positive Economics* (Chicago: University of Chicago Press, 1953).

12. See Jack Hirshleifer's "The Expanding Domain of Economics," *American Economic Review* 75, no. 8 (December 1985), pp. 53–68.

13. A frequently cited example is Armen A. Alchian, "Uncertainty, Evolution, and Economic Theory," *Journal of Political Economy* 58 (1950), pp. 211–21.

14. Edward O. Wilson, *Sociobiology* (Cambridge: Harvard University Press, 1975), p. 3.

15. *The Evolution of Cooperation* (New York: Basic Books, 1984).

16. Another example of this is what Gary Becker has called the rotten kid theorem. See his "A Theory of Social Interactions," *Journal of Political Economy* 82, no. 6 (November/December 1974), pp. 1063–93, for a discussion.

17. Recall from the chapter on empirical work the national debt controversy, for example. Robert Barro's overlapping generations model

presented in his "Are Government Bonds Net Wealth?" *Journal of Political Economy* 82 (November/December 1974), pp. 1095–1117, relies on parents having the utility of their children as an argument in the parents' utility functions.

18. See Gary Becker, "Altruism, Egoism, and Genetic Fitness: Economics and Sociobiology," *Journal of Economic Literature* 14, no. 3 (September 1976), pp. 817–26, for a model of this sort. Not everyone was convinced by Becker's explanation. See, for examples, Jack Hirshleifer, "Shakespeare vs. Becker on Altruism: The Importance of Having the Last Word," *Journal of Economic Literature* 15, no. 2 (June 1977), pp. 500–2, and Gordon Tullock, "Economics and Sociobiology: A Comment," *Journal of Economic Literature* 15, no. 2 (June 1977), pp. 502–6, as well as Becker's reply in the same issue.

19. It is worth remarking that economic theories have found themselves at least slightly applied to biological phenomena. For an interesting application see Gordon Tullock, "Biological Externalities," *Journal of Theoretical Biology* 33, no. 3 (December 1971), pp. 565–76.

20. Two examples are Marshall Jevons, *Murder at the Margin* (Sun Lakes, Ariz.: Thomas Horton and Daughters, 1978), and Murray Wolfson and Vincent Buranelli, *In the Long Run We Are All Dead* (New York: St. Martin's Press, 1984).

Chapter 12

ECONOMIC MODELS AND METHODOLOGY

This concluding chapter draws together and summarizes the material that has been presented earlier. The book has covered a wide range of topics, but all have been related to economic models and the way that economists use them. This is a methodological study because the common methodological ground that links all economists is their use of models to depict phenomena in the real world. The models themselves have a large common ground, especially in their fundamental assumptions. Because of this commonality, it is possible to characterize economics in general by the models that economists use, and it is possible to identify the differences among different schools of economic thought by the differences in the models that they use.

Studies on economic methodology could encompass much more than this, and indeed many have.[1] Because of the other excellent books on the subject, there is no reason for this study to provide another overview of the history of methodological issues in economics or the different schools of thought on the subject. The issues were raised when relevant, but this study has concentrated on examining how economists use models, and at times, how economists should use models.

This normative methodological element provides some contrast to the economic methodology that has been espoused by methodologists in the 1980s. Positivism became the reigning methodological paradigm in economics following World War II, at least in economists' words if not in their deeds, but positivism has been replaced as the methodological prescription of methodologists with methodological eclecticism. Previously, positivism was the recommended method. Now, any method is acceptable. This study has accepted the tenets of methodological eclecticism only up to a point. The main differences this study has with methodological eclecticism will be summarized again in this final chapter, for it is likely to be this message that will set this study's conclusions apart from those of its predecessors.

Another theme that reappeared throughout the book is that models, because they are simpler than the real world, can never hope to explain every real-world phenomenon. Therefore, a model that may be appropriate for one use cannot possibly be appropriate for all uses. The appropriateness of a model depends upon the specific use to which it is to be put, and one cannot judge an economic model to be an accurate representation of the real world independently of its specific application. Models appropriate for one use will necessarily be inappropriate for other uses.

Some uses of economic models were examined, ranging from standard applications like utility and entrepreneurship to more unorthodox applications like politics, animal behavior, and criminal behavior. The differences in the models can be explained by the different uses to which they are put, but the general applicability of the economic paradigm can be traced directly back to the simplicity and generality of the underlying assumptions beneath economic models of all types. The remainder of this chapter will try to tie these concepts together in more detail.

THE NATURE OF MODELS

The real world is a complex place, and it is not always easy to understand why certain things happen in the real world, why certain phenomena cause other phenomena to occur, or even whether there is a causal relationship between two phenomena. Indeed, the whole reason for scholarly inquiry is that phenomena are not easy to understand without it. One reason for this is that with many things happening at the same time, it is often difficult to isolate just those phenomena that have a cause and effect relationship. In some disciplines, controlled experiments can help, but in economics there are relatively few opportunities for controlled experiments.[2] The purpose of the model in economics, as in other disciplines, is to conceptually isolate a few phenomena so that the relationships among those phenomena can be clearly depicted in the model. The chapter on economic imperialism argued that economics has been so good at this that economic models have been applied to many phenomena outside of the normal domain of economics.

If the purpose of the model is to isolate certain phenomena by leaving much of what goes on in the real world out of the model, then the model must depict a simplified version of reality. Since everything that occurs in the real world is not included in the model, it stands to reason that one model could not possibly be appropriate for modeling all phenomena that occur in the real world. Since some things are assumed out of the model, those things assumed away cannot be depicted by the model. Therefore, the appropriateness of a model cannot be determined outside of the context in which it is used. For example, a model depicting the oil industry as competitive can do a good job of illustrating the effects of a tariff on imported oil, but it will not be able to explain why some gas stations charge different prices for gasoline than others.

This example also illustrates that it is not valid to criticize a model solely on the grounds that its assumptions are too simple. It could be valid to argue that a model is inappropriate for a particular purpose because the model has assumed away some important aspect of the real world. This is not a criticism of the model itself (which may work well when applied to a different problem), but rather a criticism of the way the model is used.

The example also illustrates that unrealistic assumptions may be appropriate under certain circumstances. Can the oil industry be depicted in a model as competitive or not? The answer to this question depends upon the particular application of the model.

REALISM IN ASSUMPTIONS

Unrealistic assumptions have been defended for decades by positivists, who argue that the test of a theory is its ability to predict and that the realism of assumptions cannot be judged outside of the context of the predictive content of the model anyway. The defense of unrealism presented here is different from the positivist defense. Unrealistic assumptions can be defended when they add to the clarity of the model, and this can occur for several reasons.[3]

The first defense of unrealistic assumptions is that the phenomena assumed away have a negligible effect on the phenomena being modeled. This type of assumption seems to most closely correspond to Friedman's idea of assumptions. For example, many economic models assume away transactions costs. Since transactions costs often have a negligible effect on the problem at hand, they may be assumed away.

A question may arise as to whether the phenomenon assumed away really does have a negligible effect, and following the positivist line of reasoning, this may be an empirical question. To continue with the same example, sometimes transactions costs are important to the phenomena being studied, and sometimes they are not and can be safely assumed away. The reason for a negligibility assumption is clarity in understanding the model. Models are simplified depictions of reality because reality is too complex to understand without limiting the study to a subset of all phenomena. Assuming away those things that have a negligible effect on the matter under study aids in understanding the real world through the model.

A second type of assumption is a domain assumption. The domain assumption implies that the model will accurately depict the real world only when the conditions specified in the domain assumption are met in the real world. For example, a model of portfolio choice might assume no inflation. This could be a negligibility assumption, as just discussed, meaning that inflation will have a negligible impact on the model's results, but it also could be a domain assumption, meaning that the model's results can be expected in the real world when there is no inflation, but will not be valid when there is inflation.

Note the crucial distinction between domain assumptions and negligibility assumptions. The negligibility assumption will assume inflation away because the model expects the same results in the real world whether there is inflation or not. The domain assumption specifies that the results of the model cannot be expected to depict real-world phenomena during inflationary times. The positivist line is that assumptions do not matter and a model is judged by its ability to predict. Considering the distinction between negligibility assumptions and domain assumptions, this clearly is not true. In the above example, the model could be used during inflationary times or noninflationary times if the assumption of no inflation is a negligibility assumption. But if it is a domain assumption, the user would expect the model not to work in inflationary times. Quite clearly, the domain assumption matters, and if the distinction is not made clear, someone could use a model that predicted well for years and then be caught unaware when, due to changing circumstances, the model no longer depicted reality.

How does one tell whether an assumption is a domain assumption or a negligibility assumption? Sometimes it may be difficult, and an assumption believed by the model builder to be a negligibility assumption may turn out to be a domain assumption. But if the distinction is never recognized, it stands no chance of being made.

The third type of assumption is the heuristic assumption. The heuristic assumption is clearly unrealistic in order to provide clarity by simplifying the understanding of the model, and turn the focus of attention to the aspects of the real world that are most important to the question at hand. For example, a model might assume a barter economy, simplifying the model but eliminating money from the analysis. This could be a domain assumption, but it also might be used as a heuristic assumption. As a heuristic assumption, it would say that even though the assumption is obviously unrealistic, including monetary exchange in the model would not affect the model's conclusions, but would make them more difficult to understand.

The ultimate conclusion is that assumptions in a model do matter. Unrealistic assumptions can be desirable for a number of reasons, but they may lead to problems—as with domain assumptions—if the reason why the unrealistic assumption works in the model is not clearly understood.

MODELS, THEORIES, ASSUMPTIONS, AND AXIOMS

An axiom is an assumption that is unquestionably accepted as true. There is a fairly constant set of axioms in economics, which typically includes utility maximization, diminishing marginal rates of substitution in consumption, and diminishing marginal productivity of variable factors of production when they are added to a fixed factor. The downward sloping demand curve is usually accepted as an axiom, although the possibility of a Giffen good may exist in theory. One reason why economic theory has been as successful as it has is that it is based on a relatively small set of axioms, and those axioms are accepted by almost all economists.

In economics, models and theories are almost interchangeable terms, because economic models without theories are not acceptable to the vast majority of current practitioners of economics. One might conjecture that a business cycle can be represented by the sum of several sine waves of different periods, but unless this model of the business cycle can be supported by a theory, economists will be reluctant to accept it, regardless of its ability to predict. Likewise, a model that relates business activity to sunspots will be slow to be accepted without a theory that can explain why sunspots would be related to business activity.[4]

Note that this is not true in other areas of inquiry, where models without theories to explain them are acceptable. If the model (such as the sine wave model above) can be validated by controlled experiment, then the model could accurately depict reality under a known set of circumstances. In economics, controlled settings are rarely possible to test such models, and the models are slow to be accepted because of the possibility of undiscovered domain assumptions, or the possibility that any correspondence between the model and the real world is due to chance. Statistically significant results at the .05 level occur one out of twenty times with random events, after all.

The theory, then, conjectures the cause and effect relationships that exist in the real world, while the model adds assumptions, explicitly and implicitly, that allow the theory to correspond to real-world phenomena. While the distinction is meaningful in an area of inquiry where models are acceptable without theories, there is little reason to make the distinction between a model and a theory in economics. The distinction may be relevant on occasion because economists are typically skeptical of models without supporting theories. Furthermore, in a positivist sense, theories are subject to empirical test. However, all theories are surrounded by a protective belt of assumptions when tested in a model, so it is the model that is tested, and assumptions will be rejected before theories are claimed to have been disproven.

FINDING THE BEST MODEL

Within economics there is a wide range of possible models that could be chosen to model any particular set of real-world phenomena. Which model is the best? The answer is that it depends upon the use to which the model will be put. As already noted, since models are simpler than the real world and always assume some things away, no model can be most appropriate for every circumstance. A model must be judged on the basis of how appropriate it is for the application, making models difficult to judge independent of an application.

In economics, as in carpentry, the results are better when the right tool is chosen for the job. Professional economists, like professional carpenters, keep a wide variety of tools, and part of the art in each case is being able to select the right tool for the application at hand.

One example of this notion was given in Chapter 9, where utility maximization could be assumed axiomatic—so that every action is utility maximizing—or it could be assumed to be consistent with some particular real-world behavior, like wealth maximization. In the latter case, the model would be more suited for yielding predictable implications, while in the former case, the model is more suited for explaining what goes on in the real world and seeking an understanding of human behavior. Another example of this can arise in choosing a general equilibrium versus a partial equilibrium model for a particular application. Which is the better approach will depend upon the application.

This does not imply, however, that any method is as good as any other in economics, or that models cannot be judged independently of their application. The next section considers this issue.

THE ISSUE OF ECLECTICISM

Methodological positivism, which has fallen out of favor with methodologists, prescribed a particular method in which theories were tested for their correspondence to the facts. While theories could not be proven true, they could be falsified, in which case they would be candidates for replacement. Methodological eclecticism replaced positivism as the methodological prescription, but eclecticism does not prescribe any particular methodology. Whatever works to uncover knowledge receives the stamp of approval from eclecticists, and since one cannot know ahead of time what might be discovered in the course of inquiry, any methodology is acceptable.

Taken completely literally, one cannot object to the eclectic view of methodology, but there are good reasons to issue some recommendations about good and bad methods. In support of eclecticism, one could not object to a particular scholar undertaking any type of inquiry in search of knowledge, and furthermore, one would not want to reject any knowledge, once discovered, because of the method that was used to discover it. There are nevertheless some recommendations that can be made with regard to method which, if they can be followed, would enhance the value of the knowledge produced.

These recommendations follow from the fact that knowledge is not developed in a vacuum. There is already a substantial body of economic knowledge on which a researcher can build, and the more closely a researcher's model adheres to the current stock of knowledge, the more reliably it can be accepted.

A recommendation from Chapter 6 is that economic models be built on individualistic foundations. The reason is that methodological individualism has stood the test of time, and for centuries has provided the foundation for a variety of different types of economic models used in various settings. Because of the success that economics as a discipline has had over the centuries in applying individualistic models, models based on individual maximizing behavior have proven themselves to be very robust. Therefore, any new discoveries made through the application of individualist models will have the advantage of resting on a foundation that has earned the confidence of economists through centuries of use.

Consider, for example, two models of the business cycle that pass the positivist test of prediction equally well. One model is based on the addition of sine waves of various periods while the other model is based on the utility maximizing behavior of individuals. Which could be the better model? While the sine wave model may eventually prove to be robust, the model based on utility maximizing behavior has a built in advantage because it uses a foundation that has proven itself in the past. Most economists would not hesitate to select the model based on utility maximization under these circumstances.

If this is so, then some methodological recommendations can be made. With regard to economic models, the primary recommendation is to choose models based on the well-established axioms of economics. The recommendation makes sense for two reasons. First, as just noted, one can have more confidence in the conclusions of a model if the model is built with parts that have proven to work well in the past. Second, economics has tremendous breadth, and any new knowledge must be integrated into the body of economics in order to be as useful as possible. Economists will have difficulty with the sine wave model alluded to above even if it proves to be more accurate than any other model because they must try to integrate this unusual model with other types of economic behavior that is depicted in a different way.

A specific subrecommendation in the category of choosing models built on well-established axioms is to build models based on the maximizing behavior of individuals. This individual maximizing behavior is accepted as axiomatic by most economists, so follows naturally. An example of problems that arise when the recommendation is not followed is the Keynesian revolution in macroeconomics. The models that seemed to predict well in the 1960s did poorly in the 1970s. In addition, economists were having trouble reconciling the body of microeconomic theory with Keynesian macroeconomics. The solution to both of these problems was to reconstruct macroeconomics in a way that was consistent with individual maximizing behavior.[5] In so doing, some of the reasons why the Keynesian models were not working well were uncovered, and macroeconomics became more consistent with microeconomics. There are many issues in macroeconomics that are far from settled, of course, but adhering to methodological individualism in the search for answers is beneficial because it has proven to be a robust foundation for economic models, and because it makes it easy to integrate new discoveries with the existing body of economics. Far from saying anything goes in methodology, then, the present study recommends methodological individualism.

The Keynesian revolution provides an example of how things can go awry in economics when the tenets of methodological individualism are not followed, but it also provides an example of the profound discoveries that can be made outside of the individualistic framework. The many contributions of Keynesian economics offer ample evidence that one would not want to reject out-of-hand any model that was not based on individual behavior. Following the tenets of eclecticism, no model should be rejected out-of-hand for methodological reasons, and no researcher should be discouraged from pursuing an unusual methodology in search of knowledge. But one must view with a skeptical eye any results that come from a model that does not rest on the proven foundation of individualism. And once a discovery is made, there is good reason to try to reconcile it with individual maximizing behavior, both as a way of increasing the confidence in the model's conclusions and as a way of integrating it in with the rest of economic knowledge.

CONCLUSION

The common ground of all of economics is its reliance on models to arrive at conclusions about the real world. Economics is at its foundation an empirical science, because its axioms are rooted in empirical observation, its models are developed with the intention of displaying a correspondence with the real world, and its conclusions are evaluated by observing the closeness of the correspondence between the model and the world. Economic models are presented in a deductive manner, deriving conclusions from a set of initial assumptions, but the development of economic knowledge is more an inductive process, where regularities are observed in the real world and models are built to try to explain those regularities.

While the common ground of economics is its reliance on models, different schools of thought part company at this point. Some economists accept utility maximization as axiomatic while others view this approach as tautological and prefer a theory which yields meaningful predictions. Some economists want to derive all of economics logically from a set of initial axioms, while others see every meaningful economic question in the real world as an empirical question. Some economists embrace mathematical models as the only way in which economic knowledge can be rigorously demonstrated, while others eschew mathematical models as meaningless tautologies.

At least part of these differences is due to the different purposes to various different schools of thought are inclined to use the models. While one would not want to claim that this would reconcile all methodological differences among economists, some progress would be made along these lines if economists recognized that different types of models were suited for different purposes, and that not all economists have the same purposes in mind.

Even recognizing these differences, there is still room to make some methodological recommendations. Methodological individualism has been noted, and the chapter on empirical work presented several suggestions for increasing the informational content of empirical results. At the close of this study it might be appropriate to consider again why an understanding of economic models and methodology would be useful. Models are the tools of economists, and one is likely to do better work if one has a better understanding of those tools.

NOTES

1. See, for examples, Mark Blaug, *The Methodology of Economics* (Cambridge: Cambridge University Press, 1980); Lawrence A. Boland, *The Foundations of Economic Method* (London: George Allen and Unwin, 1982); and Bruce J. Caldwell, *Beyond Positivism: Economic Methodology in the Twentieth Century* (London: George Allen and Unwin, 1982).

2. This is beginning to change with the establishment of a substantial group of economists pursuing experimental economics. See, for examples, Raymond C. Battalio, Leonard Green, and John H. Kagel, "Income-Leisure Tradeoffs of Animal Workers," *American Economic Review* 71, no. 4 (September 1981), pp. 621–32, and Raymond C. Battalio, John H. Kagel, Howard Rachlin, and Leonard Green, "Commodity-Choice Behavior with Pigeons as Subjects," *Journal of Political Economy* 89, no.

1 (February 1981), pp. 67–91. Experimental economics is new enough that it is not yet clear how far experimental results will generalize to the nonexperimental world.

3. The discussion here draws heavily on Alan Musgrave, " 'Unreal Assumptions' in Economic Theory: The F-Twist Untwisted," *Kyklos* 34, Fasc. 3 (1981), pp. 377–87. Some minor differences with Musgrave's presentation were discussed in Chapter 2.

4. See David Cass and Karl Shell, "Do Sunspots Matter?" *Journal of Political Economy* 91, no. 2 (April 1983), pp. 193–227.

5. Edmund S. Phelps, et al., *Microeconomic Foundations of Employment and Inflation Theory* (New York: W.W. Norton, 1970) was an important work in this regard.

BIBLIOGRAPHY

Alchian, Armen A. "Uncertainty, Evolution, and Economic Theory." *Journal of Political Economy* 58 (1950): 211–21.

Alchian, Armen A., and Harold Demsetz. "Production, Information Costs, and Economic Organization." *American Economic Review* 62 (December 1972): 777–95.

Averch, Harvey, and Leland L. Johnson. "Behavior of the Firm under Regulatory Constraint." *American Economic Review* 52, no. 5 (December 1962): 1052–69.

Axelrod, Robert. *The Evolution of Cooperation.* New York: Basic Books, 1984.

Barro, Robert J. "Are Government Bonds Net Wealth?" *Journal of Political Economy* 82 (November/December 1974): 1095–1117.

——————. "Reply to Feldstein and Buchanan." *Journal of Political Economy* 84 (April 1976): 343–49.

Bator, Francis M. "The Anatomy of Market Failure." *Quarterly Journal of Economics* 72 (August 1958): 351–79.

Battalio, Raymond C., Leonard Green, and John H. Kagel. "Income-Leisure Tradeoffs of Animal Workers." *American Economic Review* 71, no. 4 (September 1981): 621–32.

Battalio, Raymond C., John H. Kagel, Howard Rachlin, and Leonard Green. "Commodity-Choice Behavior with Pigeons as Subjects." *Journal of Political Economy* 89, no. 1 (February 1981): 67–91.

Baumol, William J. "On Method in U.S. Economics a Century Earlier." *American Economic Review* 75, no. 6 (December 1985): 1–12.

Baumol, William J., and Alan S. Blinder. *Economics: Principles and Policy,* 2d ed. New York: Harcourt Brace Jovanovich, Inc., 1982.

Becker, Gary S. "Altruism, Egoism, and Genetic Fitness: Economics and Sociobiology." *Journal of Economic Literature* 14, no. 3 (September 1976): 817–26.

——————. *The Economic Approach to Human Behavior.* Chicago: University of Chicago Press, 1976.

——————. *Economic Theory.* New York: Alfred A. Knopf, 1971.

————. "Reply to Hirshleifer and Tullock." *Journal of Economic Literature* 15, no. 2 (June 1977): 506–7.

————. "A Theory of Social Interactions." *Journal of Political Economy* 82, no. 6 (November/December 1974): 1063–93.

————. *Treatise on the Family*. Cambridge, Mass.: Harvard University Press, 1981.

Benson, Bruce, M. L. Greenhut, and Randall G. Holcombe. "Interest Groups and the Antitrust Paradox." *Cato Journal* 6, no. 3 (Winter 1987): 801–17.

Blaug, Mark. *The Methodology of Economics*. Cambridge: Cambridge University Press, 1980.

Boland, Lawrence A. *The Foundations of Economic Method*. London: George Allen and Unwin, 1982.

Born, Max. *Einstein's Theory of Relativity*. New York: Dover, 1962.

Boudreaux, Donald J., and Randall G. Holcombe. "The Coasian and Knightian Theories of the Firm." *Managerial and Decision Economics* (forthcoming, 1989).

Brock, William A. "Contestable Markets and the Theory of Industry Structure." *Journal of Political Economy* 91, no. 6 (December 1983): 1055–66.

Broad, C. D. *The Philosophy of Francis Bacon*. Cambridge: Cambridge University Press, 1926.

Buchanan, James M. "Barro on the Ricardian Equivalence Theorem." *Journal of Political Economy* 84 (April 1976): 337–42.

————. "Public Finance and Public Choice." *National Tax Journal* 28 (December 1975): 383–94.

————. "What Should Economists Do?" *Southern Economic Journal* 30, no. 3 (January 1964): 213–22.

————. *What Should Economists Do?* Indianapolis: Liberty Press, 1979.

Buchanan, James M., and Gordon Tullock. *The Calculus of Consent*. Ann Arbor: University of Michigan Press, 1962.

Buchanan, James M., and Richard E. Wagner. *Democracy in Deficit: The Political Legacy of Lord Keynes*. New York: Academic Press, 1977.

Butos, William N. "Hayek and General Equilibrium Analysis." *Southern Economic Journal* 52, no. 2 (October 1985): 332–43.

Caldwell, Bruce J. *Beyond Positivism: Economic Methodology in the Twentieth Century*. London: George Allen and Unwin, 1982.

Caldwell, Bruce J., and A.W. Coats. "The Rhetoric of Economists: A Comment on McClosky." *Journal of Economic Literature* 22, no. 2 (June 1984): 575–78.

Caudill, Steven B., and Randall G. Holcombe. "Coefficient Bias Due to

Specification Search in Econometric Models." *Atlantic Economic Journal* 15, no. 3 (September 1987): 30–34.

Cass, David, and Karl Shell. "Do Sunspots Matter?" *Journal of Political Economy* 91, no. 2 (April 1983): 193–227.

Clower, Robert W. "The Keynesian Counter-Revolution: A Theoretical Appraisal." Chapter 19 in R. W. Clower, ed. *Monetary Theory*. Baltimore: Penguin, 1969.

Coase, Ronald H. "The Nature of the Firm." In George J. Stigler and Kenneth E. Boulding, eds., *Readings in Price Theory*. Chicago: Richard D. Irwin, 1952, pp. 331–51.

Cooley, Thomas F., and Stephen F. LeRoy. "Identification and Estimation of Money Demand." *American Economic Review* 71, no. 5 (December 1981): 825–44.

Denton, Frank T. "Data Mining as an Industry." *Review of Economics and Statistics* 68, no. 1 (February 1985): 124–27.

Downs, Anthony. *An Economic Theory of Democracy*. New York: Harper and Row, 1957.

Ehrlich, Isaac. "The Deterrent Effect of Capital Punishment: A Question of Life and Death." *American Economic Review* 65, no. 3 (June 1975): 397–417.

Evans, Paul. "Do Large Deficits Produce High Interest Rates?" *American Economic Review* 75, no. 1 (March 1985): 68–87.

Feldstein, Martin. "Government Deficits and Aggregate Demand." *Journal of Monetary Economics* 9 (1982): 1–20.

———. "Perceived Wealth in Bonds and Social Security: A Comment." *Journal of Political Economy* 84 (April 1976): 331–36.

Ferguson, C. E. *Microeconomic Theory*, Revised Edition. Homewood, Illinois: Irwin, 1969.

Foley, Duncan K., and Miguel Sidrauski. *Monetary and Fiscal Policy in a Growing Economy*. New York: Macmillan, 1971.

Freyerabend, Paul. *Against Method*. Atlantic Highlands: Humanities Press, 1975.

Friedman, Milton. *Essays in Positive Economics*. Chicago: University of Chicago Press, 1953.

———. "The Marshallian Demand Curve." *Journal of Political Economy* 57, no. 6 (December 1949): 463–95.

———. *Price Theory: A Provisional Text*, Revised Edition. Chicago: Aldine, 1962.

———. "Right at Last, an Expert's Dream." *Newsweek* (March 10, 1986): 8.

———. "The Role of Monetary Policy." *American Economic Review* 58, no. 1 (March 1968): 1–17.

Gwartney, James D., and Richard Stroup. *Economics: Private and Public Choice*, 3d ed. New York: Academic Press, 1982.

――――. "Labor Supply and Tax Rates: A Correction of the Record." *American Economic Review* 73, no. 3 (June 1983): 446–51.

Hayek, Friedrich A. *Monetary Theory and the Trade Cycle*. New York: Augustus M. Kelley, 1966.

――――. *Studies in Philosophy, Politics, and Economics*. Chicago: University of Chicago Press, 1967.

Hesse, Mary B. *Models and Analogies in Science*. Notre Dame, Indiana: University of Notre Dame Press, 1966.

Hirshleifer, Jack. "The Expanding Domain of Economics." *American Economic Review* 75, no. 6 (December 1985): 53–68.

――――. "Shakespeare vs. Becker on Altruism: The Importance of Having the Last Word." *Journal of Economic Literature* 15, no. 2 (June 1977): 500–502.

Hicks, John R. "The Mainspring of Economic Growth." *American Economic Review* 71, no. 6 (December 1981): 23–29.

Hoaglin, David C., Frederick Mosteller, and John W. Tukey. *Exploring Data Tables, Trends, and Shapes*. New York: John Wiley & Sons, 1985.

――――. *Understanding Robust and Exploratory Data Analysis*. New York: John Wiley & Sons, 1983.

Holcombe, Randall G. "Concepts of Public Sector Equilibrium." *National Tax Journal* 33, no. 1 (March 1980): 77–88.

――――. *Public Finance and the Political Process*. Carbondale: Southern Illinois University Press, 1983.

Holcombe, Randall, John Jackson, and Asghar Zardkoohi. "The National Debt Controversy." *Kyklos* 34, Fasc. 2 (1981): 186–202.

Hoover, Kevin D. "Two Types of Monetarism." *Journal of Economic Literature* 22, no. 1 (March 1984): 58–76.

Jensen, Michael, and William Meckling. "The Theory of the Firm: Managerial Behavior, Agency Costs, and Ownership Structure." *Journal of Financial Economics* 3 (October 1976): 305–60.

Jevons, Marshall. *Murder at the Margin*. Sun Lakes, Ariz.: Thomas Horton and Daughters, 1978.

Jevons, W. Stanley. *The Principles of Science*. London: MacMillan and Co., 1887.

Kagel, John H., Raymond C. Battalio, Howard Rachlin, Leonard Green, Robert L. Basmann, and W. R. Klem. "Experimental Studies of Consumer Demand Using Laboratory Animals." *Economic Inquiry* 13 (March 1975): 22–38.

Kaldor, Nicholas. "The Irrelevance of Equilibrium Economics." *Econom-

ic Journal 82 (December 1972): 1237–55.

Kaplan, Abraham. *The Conduct of Inquiry: Methodology for Behavioral Science*. San Francisco: Chandler, 1964.

Katz, Jerrold J. *The Problem of Induction and Its Solution*. Chicago: University of Chicago Press, 1962.

Keynes, John Maynard. *The General Theory of Employment, Interest, and Money*. New York: Harcourt, Brace, 1936.

Kirzner, Israel M. *Competition and Entrepreneurship*. Chicago: University of Chicago Press, 1973.

————. *The Economic Point of View*. Kansas City: Sheed and Ward, Inc., 1976.

Knight, Frank H. "Profits and Entrepreneurial Functions." *Journal of Economic History*, vol. 2 supplement (December 1942): 126–32.

————. *Risk, Uncertainty, and Profit*. Boston: Houghton Mifflin, 1921.

Kochin, Levis A. "Are Future Taxes Anticipated by Consumers?" *Journal of Money, Credit, and Banking* 6, no. 3 (August 1974): 385–94.

Kormendi, Roger C. "Government Debt, Government Spending, and Private Sector Behavior." *American Economic Review* 73, no. 5 (December 1983): 994–1010.

Kuhn, Thomas S. *The Structure of Scientific Revolutions*. Chicago: University of Chicago Press, 1962.

Lakatos, Imre. *The Methodology of Scientific Research Programmes*, vol. I. Cambridge: Cambridge University Press, 1978.

Leamer, Edward E. "Let's Take the Con out of Econometrics." *American Economic Review* 73, no. 1 (1983): 31–43.

————. "Sensitivity Analysis Would Help." *American Economic Review* 75, no. 3 (June 1985): 308–13.

Leatherdale, W. H. *The Role of Analogy, Model, and Metaphor in Science*. Amsterdam: North Holland, 1974.

Leijonhufvud, Axel. *On Keynesian Economics and the Economics of Keynes*. London: Oxford University Press, 1968.

Lipsey, Robert. "The Relationship Between Unemployment and the Rate of Change of Money Wage Rates in the United Kingdom, 1862–1957: A Further Analysis." *Economica* 27 (February 1960): 1–31.

Lovell, Michael C. "Data Mining." *Review of Economics and Statistics* 65, no. 1 (February 1983): 1–12.

Lucas, Robert E., Jr. "Econometric Policy Evaluation: A Critique." Pp. 19–46 in Karl Brunner and Alan H. Meltzer, eds., *The Phillips Curve and Labor Markets*. Amsterdam: North Holland, 1976.

————. "An Equilibrium Model of the Business Cycle." *Journal of Political Economy* 83, no. 6 (December 1975): 1133–44.

———. *Studies in Business Cycle Theory*. Cambridge, Mass.: MIT Press, 1981.

———. "Understanding Business Cycles." Pp. 7–30 in Karl Brunner and Alan H. Meltzer, eds., *Stabilization of the Domestic and International Economy*. Amsterdam: North Holland, 1977.

Mayer, Thomas. "Economics as a Hard Science: Realistic Goal or Wishful Thinking." *Economic Inquiry* 18, no. 2 (April 1980): 165–78.

McAleer, Michael, Adrian R. Pagan, and Paul A. Volker. "What Will Take the Con Out of Econometrics?" *American Economic Review* 75, no. 3 (June 1985): 293–307.

McCloskey, Donald M. "The Loss Function Has Been Mislaid: The Rhetoric of Significance Tests." *American Economic Review* 75, no. 2 (May 1985): 201–5.

———. "Reply to Caldwell and Coats." *Journal of Economic Literature* 22, no. 2 (June 1984): 579–80.

———. "The Rhetoric of Economics." *Journal of Economic Literature* 21, no. 7 (June 1983): 481–517.

———. *The Rhetoric of Economics*. Madison: University of Wisconsin Press, 1985.

McKenzie, Richard B. "The Neoclassicalists vs. the Austrians: A Partial Reconciliation of Competing Worldviews." *Southern Economic Journal* 47, no. 1 (July 1980): 1–13.

———. "The Non-Rational Domain and the Limits of Economic Analysis." *Southern Economic Journal* 46, no. 1 (July 1979): 145–57.

Meyer, Werner. "Snake Oil Salesmen." *Policy Review* 37 (Summer 1986): 74–77.

Mises, Ludwig von. *Epistemological Problems of Economics*. New York: New York University Press, 1981.

———. *Human Action: A Treatise on Economics*, 3rd. rev. ed. Chicago: Henry Regnery Company, 1966.

———. *The Ultimate Foundation of Economic Science*. Kansas City: Sheed Andrews and McMeel, Inc., 1978, originally published 1962.

Morey, Edward R. "Confuser Surplus." *American Economic Review* 74, no. 1 (March 1984): 163–73.

Mosteller, Frederick, and John W. Tukey. *Data Analysis and Regression*. Reading, Mass.: Addison-Wesley, 1977.

Musgrave, Alan. " 'Unreal Assumptions' in Economic Theory: The F-Twist Untwisted." *Kyklos* 34, Fasc. 3 (1981): 377–87.

Muth, John F. "Rational Expectations and the Theory of Price Movements." *Econometrica* 29, no. 6 (July 1961): 315–35.

Nozick, Robert. *Philosophical Explanations*. Cambridge, Mass.: Belknap, 1981.

O'Driscoll, Gerald P., Jr., and Mario J. Rizzo. *The Economics of Time and Ignorance*. Oxford: Basil Blackwell Ltd, 1985.

Phelps, Edmund S., et al. *Microeconomic Foundations of Employment and Inflation Theory*. New York: W. W. Norton, 1970.

Phillips, A.W. "The Relation Between Unemployment and the Rate of Change of Money Wage Rates in the United Kingdom, 1862–1957." *Economica* 25 (November 1958): 283–99.

Popper, Karl R. *The Logic of Scientific Discovery*. New York: Basic Books, 1959.

Posner, Richard A. *Economic Analysis of Law*. Boston: Little, Brown, 1972.

Priest, George L. "The Common Law Process and the Selection of Legal Rules." *Journal of Legal Studies* 6, no. 1 (January 1977): 65–82.

Reid, Bradford G. "Aggregate Consumption and Deficit Financing: An Attempt to Separate Permanent from Transitory Effects." *Economic Inquiry* 23, No. 3 (July 1985): 475–86.

Ricketts, Martin. "Tax Theory and Tax Policy." Pp. 29–46 in Alan Peacock and Francesco Forte, eds., *The Political Economy of Taxation*. New York: St. Martin's Press, 1981.

Rizzo, Mario J. "Praxeology and Econometrics: A Critique of Positivist Economics." In Louis M. Spadaro, ed., *New Directions in Austrian Economics*. Kansas City: Sheed Andrews and McMeel, Inc., 1978.

Robbins, Lionel. *An Essay on the Nature and Significance of Economic Science*. London: MacMillan and Co., 1935.

Rothbard, Murray N. *Man, Economy, and State*. Los Angeles: Nash, 1962.

Rubin, Paul H. "Why Is the Common Law Efficient?" *Journal of Legal Studies* 6, no. 1 (January 1977): 51–63.

Samuelson, Paul A. *Foundations of Economic Analysis*. Cambridge, Mass.: Harvard University Press, 1947.

———. "Maximum Principles in Analytical Economics." *American Economic Review* 62, no. 3 (June 1972): 249–62.

———. "My Life Philosophy." *The American Economist* 27, no. 2 (Fall 1983): 5–12.

Samuelson, Paul A., and Robert M. Solow. "Analytical Aspects of Anti-inflation Policy." *American Economic Review* 50, no. 2 (May 1960): 177–94.

Scherer, F. M. *Industrial Market Structure and Economic Performance*. Chicago: Rand McNally & Co., 1970.

Seater, John J. "Are Future Taxes Discounted?" *Journal of Money, Credit, and Banking* 14 (August 1982): 376–89.

Sraffa, Piero. "The Laws of Returns Under Competitive Conditions." *Economic Journal* 36 (December 1926): 535–50.

Stigler, George J. "The Division of Labor Is Limited by the Extent of the Market." *Journal of Political Economy* (June 1951): 185–93, reprinted in William Breit and Harold M. Hochman, eds., *Readings in Microeconomics*, 2d ed. New York: Holt, Rinehart, and Winston, 1971, pp. 140–48.

———. "The Economics of Information." *Journal of Political Economy* 69 (June 1961): 213–25.

———. "The Theory of Economic Regulation." *Bell Journal of Economics and Management Science* 2 (Spring 1971): 3–21.

Stigler, George J., and Gary S. Becker. "De Gustibus Non Est Disputandum." *American Economic Review* 67, no. 2 (March 1977): 76–90.

Tanner, J. Earnest. "An Empirical Investigation of Tax Discounting." *Journal of Money, Credit, and Banking* 11, no. 2 (May 1979): 214–18.

———. "Fiscal Policy and Consumer Behavior." *Review of Economics and Statistics* 61, no. 2 (May 1979): 317–21.

Tukey, John W. *Exploratory Data Analysis*. Reading, Mass.: Addison-Wesley, 1977.

Tullock, Gordon. "Biological Externalities." *Journal of Theoretical Biology* 33, no. 3 (December 1971): 565–76.

———. "Economics and Sociobiology: A Comment." *Journal of Economic Literature* 15, no. 2 (June 1977): 502–506.

———. *The Organization of Inquiry*. Durham, N.C.: Duke University Press, 1966.

———. "Publication Decisions and Tests of Significance." *Journal of the American Statistical Association* 54 (September 1959): 593.

Velleman, Paul F., and David C. Hoaglin. *Applications, Basics, and Computing of Exploratory Data Analysis*. Boston: Duxbury Press, 1981.

Wilson, Edward O. *Sociobiology*. Cambridge, Mass.: Harvard University Press, 1975.

Wolfson, Murray, and Vincent Buranelli. *In the Long Run We Are All Dead*. New York: St. Martin's Press, 1984.

Wulwick, Nancy J. "The Phillips Curve: Which? Whose? To Do What? How?" *Southern Economic Journal* 53, no. 4 (April 1987): 834–857.

Young, Allyn A. "Increasing Returns and Economic Progress." *Economic Journal* 38 (December 1928): 527–42.

INDEX

About the Author

RANDALL G. HOLCOMBE is Professor of Economics at Florida State University, Tallahassee. He has written *Public Finance and the Political Process, An Economic Analysis of Democracy,* and *Public Sector Economics,* as well as numerous articles.